Privatization and Development

PRIVATIZATION AND DEVELOPMENT

Edited by
Steve H. Hanke

338·93

A Publication of the
INTERNATIONAL CENTER FOR ECONOMIC GROWTH
ICS PRESS

Institute for Contemporary Studies
San Francisco, California

Inquiries, book orders, and catalog requests should be addressed to International Center for Economic Growth, 243 Kearny Street, San Francisco, CA 94108 (415) 981-5353.

Book design and production by Marian Hartsough

Many of the papers in this book were delivered in a slightly different form at a conference on privatization sponsored by the United States Agency for International Development and conducted by the Sequoia Institute in Washington, D.C. in February, 1986. This publication was funded by U.S.A.I.D.

PDC-0092-I-00-4047-07

U.S.A.I.D.

Contents

Part V
Cases of Privatization

Part VI
Conclusion

Preface

In the past several years, interest in privatization—which means contracting with or selling to private parties the functions or firms previously controlled or owned by governments—has been growing in both
developed and developing countries. There are many reasons for this,
but the most important have to do with a combination of growing pressures on public budgets and mounting evidence that the competitive
discipline of private markets increases efficiency, producing greater quality at a lower cost. Even the socialist countries have thus been affected
by the movement, and pressures for privatization have surfaced in almost
all of the Eastern Bloc countries.

Privatization has also become a policy "growth area" because of
the *form* it has taken—in distinct contrast to past government efforts
to "denationalize" public enterprises. A major impulse to nationalize
private firms has come from the belief—whether mistaken or not—
that the existence of large private firms concentrate power and wealth
in the hands of the few and thus obstruct the commitments of many
countries to equality. Where this perception has been strong, as in Britain for instance, denationalization was simply seen as a step backward,
toward reconcentration of wealth. On the other hand, privatization,

at least as it has occurred in many countries, has changed the perceptions of many people toward private ownership by consciously implementing the sale of firms to large numbers of individual shareholders.

The broadening of private ownership has important political implications, and also accords in a significant and interesting way with the International Center for Economic Growth's (ICEG) special interest in human development. In Britain, where the movement has been particularly strong, this aspect of privatization has stimulated a "people's capitalism," which has produced strong political constituencies for private ownership even among Labor Party voters.

While it is obviously impossible to know whether interest in privatization will continue, it is nevertheless a subject of great current interest in many places. This book, edited by Steve H. Hanke, is the result of a conference on privatization sponsored by the United States Agency for International Development held in Washington, D.C. in February 1986. The conference, as the papers in this volume show, considered a broad series of issues related to privatization and explored practical approaches drawn from real country experiences with it.

This book is meant to be a "how-to" manual on techniques of privatization. It is our first publication on this important subject, which will be an ongoing concern for the Center as it explores new development strategies.

NICOLAS ARDITO BARLETTA
Director
International Center for Economic Growth

Panama City
October, 1987

Acknowledgments

I want to express my appreciation for the assistance provided by the Sequoia Institute in the preparation of this volume. Wendy Jordan prepared much of the conference transcripts for publication; Jerry Jenkins provided many hours of valuable conversation on the subject matter. Dr. Jenkins epitomizes the best qualities of any "think tank."

I wish also to thank the following persons from the Agency for International Development for their work on the International Conference on Privatization and the preparation of this book: Jay F. Morris, Deputy Administrator; Neal Peden, Assistant Administrator, Bureau for Private Enterprise (PRE); Richard E. Bissell, Assistant Administrator, Bureau for Program and Policy Coordination (PPC); Richard A. Derham, former Assistant Administrator, PPC; Anabel Smith, former Special Assistant to the Assistant Administrator, PRE; Douglas Trussell, Special Assistant to the Assistant Administrator, PRE; and Neal S. Zank, Senior Policy Advisor for Private Enterprise, PPC.

Finally, I wish to thank the staff of the Institute for Contemporary Studies, especially A. Lawrence Chickering, its executive editor, and Robert W. Davis, who assisted in the editing of this volume.

—S.H.H.

Part I

Privatization in the
Developing World

1

Steve H. Hanke

Introduction

In developed and developing countries alike, privatization is one of the most revolutionary innovations in the recent history of economic policy. Margaret Thatcher has made it a central part of her economic policy in Great Britain; last November the French embarked on a program to sell off sixty-five state-owned companies and banks; and major privatization programs are underway in developing countries everywhere. Even the "People's Republics" of Africa—countries such as Angola, Benin, the Congo, and Tanzania—have begun turning to private-sector management of inefficient state-owned firms.

The popularity of privatization has different origins, reflecting different hopes that its proponents have for it. Many proponents emphasize efficiency. They see privatization as a means to increase output, improve quality, and reduce unit costs. Others hope it will curb the growth of public spending and raise cash to reduce government debt. Others like its general emphasis on private initiative and private markets as the most successful route to economic growth and human development. Finally, a large group sees in privatization a way to broaden the base of ownership and participation in a society— encouraging larger numbers to feel they have a stake in the system.

Privatization is the transfer of assets and service functions from public to private hands. It includes, therefore, activities that range from selling state-owned enterprises to contracting out public services with private contractors. In a country like the United States, where few economic sectors—with the important exception of land, minerals, energy, and timber resources—are owned by the government, privatization has tended to be limited to contracting out public services. In developed countries such as Britain and France, however, as well as in most developing countries, the government owns a large fraction of the nation's industrial enterprises; and in most of the world, therefore, large opportunities for privatization exist in outright sale of publicly owned and operated firms. Such sales have in fact characterized much of the move toward privatization in many places.

The issues related to privatization are many. Besides broad issues of economics, privatization raises issues of finance (what financial strategy should be adopted to accomplish a particular privatization objective?), property rights and law (is the legal structure, especially as it relates to property rights, adequate to support successful privatization?), tax structure (does the tax system encourage private equity ownership?), and especially politics. In some ways, of course, the last of these issues is the most important, since political factors will ultimately determine whether a venture in privatization can be tried. Therefore, a critical part of any privatization strategy requires thinking through a plan that will mobilize coalitions in favor of privatization to overcome expected opposition from interest groups.

This book is meant to be a "handbook" on privatization. The papers in it were presented at a major conference on privatization, which took place in February 1986 in Washington, D. C. The conference, which was sponsored by the U. S. Agency for International Development (AID) and organized by the Sequoia Institute, was noteworthy for several reasons. First, the more than 500 participants that attended from all over the world represented a wide and rare spectrum of professions, viewpoints, and countries. Rarely have such a diverse group of scholars, politicians, public-sector bureaucrats, and private investors joined in such an effort. The conference was also interesting as its central purpose represented an implicit critique of some of AID's own past policies, and it spoke with the increasing voice of recognition that good economic policies are more important than any form of aid in encouraging economic and social development.

The papers in this volume are organized to address practical problems facing countries which are pursuing, or would like to pursue, privatization strategies. The first section looks at the foundations — the broad issues of economics, law, and politics — which must be central to any privatization effort. The second addresses the crucial issue of planning. The third examines privatization in the context of development and explores opportunities for privatization in developing countries. And the fourth then considers four specific case studies, taken from both developed and developing countries.

The authors present wide-ranging discussions of both theoretical and practical aspects of privatization. In the face of overwhelming evidence of failure in traditional development strategies, privatization offers an important opportunity to move in new directions. In the chapters that follow, the authors explore the challenge of privatization — both the opportunities and the pitfalls associated with it.

2

L. Gray Cowan

A Global Overview
of Privatization

Worldwide interest in reducing the role of the public sector in national economies is a phenomenon of the past four to six years. The growing movement to privatize industries, services, and agencies and the changed conception of government's role are products of pragmatism: the state-owned sector is not working, and enormous subsidies to maintain money-losing enterprises and services only get bigger. The conviction is growing that private entrepreneurs can manage industries more effectively and operate services more efficiently and at lower cost to the public than can the government. Evidence supporting private enterprise over public ownership has emerged in areas of every continent. This paper summarizes some of the current endeavors and successes of different regions.

Europe

Much has been said of the shining example of privatization provided
by the Thatcher government in Great Britain. Motivated by the desire
to promote public share ownership in divested state enterprises and
to introduce competition and market discipline into fields that had been
monopolized by the government, Thatcher's administration believes
privatization will bring both greater efficiency and widespread consumer benefits. The program has resulted in more than 850,000 tenants becoming owners of houses formerly owned by local government
authorities; majority private control of British Telecommunications
achieved through share offering in a flotation surpassed in size only
by the sale of British Gas Corporation two years later; and disposal
of a variety of other enterprises ranging from road haulage to hotels
to an automobile plant. The new shareholders of British Telecom realized an immediate profit on their holdings, and telephone service has
improved substantially under private management. Complete privatization, combined with reduction of the government's share in other
enterprises, netted nearly $30 billion within the eighteen months fol-
lowing divestment.

During 1985 and 1986, Rolls Royce, British Gas Corporation, British Airways, and several airports were privatized. London's "big bang"
no-holds-barred competition in financial markets broke up the nation's
securities monopoly, and has thus been termed "stocks for the masses."
Even electrical power, long considered a natural monopoly, is under
consideration for privatization. The 1983 Energy Act permits private
firms to commission and run their own power stations, and several companies are interested in doing so. All in all, government tax incentives,
employee stock ownership plans, and continued, highly successful
privatization have more than trebled the number of British stockholders
since the Tory victory in 1983.

Privatization is on the agenda of other European countries, though
not everywhere to the degree envisaged in Britain. In Italy, efforts are
being made to overcome the multibillion-dollar annual losses of the
government-owned holding companies IRI, which owns Alfa Romeo,
through the auctioning of parts of IRI. In addition, in June 1985 the

Italian government held a stock sale of Sirti, a profitable telecommunications company that then netted more than $500 million in less than a year; the government also sold 20 percent equity in Italy's state airline. Like Great Britain, Italy has opened up its financial market: Consob, the Italian stock exchange, demands that listed companies sell a minimum of 25 percent of their shares to the public as a condition of being quoted on the stock exchange.

To reduce its losses, Spain's National Industrial Institute has been ordered to reduce sharply the number of companies it controls. The government plans to privatize national energy holdings and is luring foreign interests from the United States, Japan, and the rest of Europe. In 1985, West Germany stated plans for initial privatization activities. Deregulation and the arrival of international investment banks have opened up the bond market, though foreign investors are not entirely assimilated.

French privatization was launched in November 1986, only eight months after the election of a conservative parliament. Projects have included a public offering of 50 percent of Saint Gobain, a state-owned glass and special materials group. It's interesting to note that when trading opened a month after the offering, shares were placed 18 percent above offer price. Premier Jacques Chirac's early move to replace the chiefs of more than a dozen state-owned banks and companies with private enterprise sympathizers drew sharp criticism, but the country's denationalization program is gaining momentum as several interests are targeted: the state insurance company (Assurances Générales de France); CGCT (Compagnie Générale de Constructions Téléphoniques), a state-owned deficit-running telecommunications company that supplies 16 percent of public sector and 25 percent of private telecommunications equipment. Chirac also plans to sell French interests in television.

Turkey has extensive plans for privatization and the necessary legislation in place to dispose of a number of state enterprises, but results thus far are limited to the sale of toll-collection rights for a Bosporus bridge and the Keban Dam. Currently for sale are state-owned cement and fertilizer companies, among others. For some time Canada has been in the process of reducing the government's stake in some of its

Crown Corporations by selling them to the private sector; in particular, the conglomerate Canada Development Corporation is now almost entirely in private hands. In the past year, completed sales include Canadair Limited (the state aircraft maker), some mines, two transport development companies, and an airline.

Privatization in Britain and elsewhere has not been without its critics. The British government has been accused of selling national assets simply as a means of increasing revenues to avoid the politically unpleasant necessity of raising tax rates. The parliamentary opposition has vowed to reverse privatization if it should come to power; but as the election of June 1987 shows, the political constituency that benefits from privatization continues to grow, and it will be increasingly difficult and costly to revert to government ownership.

The Less-Developed Countries

Increasing interest in privatization in the LDCs is reflected in the growing number of requests for advice and assistance received over the past three years by the missions of the United States Agency for International Development in establishing privatization plans. Indicative of LDC concern are the figures that emerged from a cable sent by the U.S. Department of the Treasury to all embassies and missions in April 1985 seeking information on the status of privatization efforts at each post. All but four of the nearly sixty replies received indicated that divestment and privatization of state-owned industries and services was of concern to their governments. The reason for interest most often cited was the untenable financial pressures exerted by continued subsidies. It was evident from the replies that one of the major obstacles to more rapid privatization was simply a lack of knowledge about how to go about the process.

All too often, governments see divestment as the simple process of announcing a willingness to sell and finding a suitable buyer at a price the government is willing to accept. One of the more difficult tasks facing the missions is to convince LDC governments that privatization can often be a slow, frustrating activity.

Hand in hand with privatization go assistance in developing capital markets, provision of credit facilities, and reform of macroeconomic policies so that the private sector can expand. Governments must be made aware that little will be gained from privatization if industries are protected from market forces. In some countries the private sector is not sufficiently developed to provide the domestic financing necessary to buy state-owned firms. And there may be resistance to allowing sales to private foreign investors where this is seen as leading toward loss of national control over industrial development. Governments need to be assured that this need not be the case. Examples of successful joint ventures can be cited to allay these fears. Following are examples of some of the projects that have been undertaken.

Asia

With some exceptions, privatization in the developing world has been hampered by the lack of capital markets, especially legal ones, and by severely limited credit facilities available to the private sector. Privatization cannot take place unless there is enough capital in private hands to provide potential buyers for state divestiture. Substantial progress has been made in Southeast Asia in developing sophisticated financial institutions; consequently, privatization has made correspondingly greater progress there than in the rest of the developing world. A second major difficulty faced by many countries is that there is no real knowledge of the extent of the public sector: commitments have been made by numerous ministries, without central coordination, and as a result the government may find itself with a financial interest in enterprises over which it has exercised no control.

In Southeast Asia, Malaysia has shown an especially strong interest in privatization, in part because of the examples furnished by Singapore and Hong Kong, and in part because of the Prime Minister's interest. The government sold a minority interest in Malaysian Airlines System and expects to relinquish majority control by 1988. After revamping the fleet of the Malaysian International Shipping Company, the government partially privatized it in late 1986, and facilities at Port

Klang have also been sold to the private sector. Maintenance of the Malaysian national air force is privatized. Much more ambitious is the proposed divestment of the national telecommunications system, using the British example. In this case as in others where international business is developing rapidly, the government is faced with the prospect of investing heavily in the modernization of the national communications system or having business bypass it for more efficient private systems. Privatization is the logical alternative.

Thailand plans to privatize its telecommunications system as well as its railroads and municipal transport systems, but these plans have not yet come to fruition. The government has resolved to curtail its involvement in the oil sector as well. Formation of a privatization plan is now under consideration. The Philippines government has launched a program to sell 36 companies owned by the National Development Corporation, including refining and marketing companies, that were taken over to prevent their collapse when they failed under private management. President Aquino completely dismantled the energy ministry during her early months in power, indicating her dedication to limited state control.

Among the less-developed nations in the area, Bangladesh has taken a major step toward returning to private ownership the jute mills, which were nationalized more than a decade ago. More than 400 public sector assets have been divested, including newspapers, a fishing fleet, chemical- and food-processing plants, and 8 percent of the government-owned steel and engineering corporation. Four of the six nationalized commercial banks were sold to the private sector. Since 1982 the country has begun deregulation of investment. Since the 1970s the number of state-owned enterprises (SOEs) has dropped from 90 percent of industrial assets to 40 percent. Food subsidies dropped from 12.5 to 8.5 percent of the national budget between 1978 and 1985; during the same period agricultural subsidies dropped from 10 to 2.4 percent.

In the Far East, Japan has reduced its comparatively small public sector with the partial sale of Nippon Telegraph & Telephone, and it plans to sell the national airline, railways, and the tobacco monopoly. The government expects that competition will make these firms more efficient and profitable. Finally, under the guise of improving socialism, the People's Republic of China has initiated widespread reforms in agriculture and industry aimed at improving individual incentive and industrial productivity.

Latin America

Privatization has had a somewhat checkered history in Latin America. In Chile, the military government has long been committed to privatization: more than a decade ago the bulk of state-owned firms was sold to the private sector, and the public school system was privatized. The results were not always good; many firms failed and had to be rescued by the government. The experiment has served to strengthen the private sector, however, and has led to the establishment of private pension funds alongside the existing state fund.

In Mexico, President de la Madrid's government announced the divestment of 236 state-owned companies early in his term, but thus far fewer than fifty have been put up for sale (although these include important hotels and auto-making firms). Questions have been raised about the seriousness of the government's intent, since sale of some obvious candidates has been refused based on the familiar argument of strategic importance to national security. A major move was the introduction of debt-free equity in the summer of 1986, equity with about $700 million already approved and $500 million in processing. The program is considered a resounding success.

In Argentina, the civilian government is developing plans for privatization, but they are at an initial stage. The YPF would like to transfer some producing oil fields but the terms are still undecided, and some chemical assets have been put up for sale. In late 1986 President Raúl Alfonsín launched a program of improvement that includes reducing his central administration, and he developed a holding company to run state enterprises by more market-oriented principles in tariffs and employment. The law requires special congressional authorization for the sale of major state companies (including YPF), but not for the sale of a number of mixed capital enterprises.

Honduras, Belize, and Jamaica have all tackled privatization aggressively during the past two years. A variety of divestitures and leasing arrangements have been developed across a wide range of industries and service sectors.

Africa

Privatization on the African continent has been progressing more slowly in part because of financial constraints, a lack of how-to knowledge, and political hesitation by governments. In only three cities of sub-Saharan Africa — Abidjan, Nairobi, and Harare — can there be said to exist a fledgling capital market. The pressure on governments to reduce the burden of subsidies is growing; in some cases African governments have been refused loans from commercial banks because their portfolios are entirely committed to servicing the debt and operating subsidies of the public sector.

In West Africa, Togo has made the most energetic efforts toward privatization. Run by a military dictatorship, the country is extremely stable politically though it is one of the world's poorest nations. It has no stock exchange, so SOE sales are conducted through government negotiations. Buyers were first offered leasing deals, which require less capital outlay than outright purchase; then sales of assets became possible. Under the direction of the minister of state enterprises, all of the country's fifty-eight public sector enterprises are up for disposal. The first project was the sale of the state steel company, then the state oil refining and storage unit was leased to a private U.S. firm. The government has contracted European managers for some enterprises. Currently for sale are a recording studio, a trucking firm, and a salt-producing company.

Some question the wisdom of selling the state assets of developing countries to foreign investors, but a good sign for Togo's economy is the flight of capital from neighboring countries increasingly directed into Lome, the nation's capital. Privatization is only one element of a national economic policy that is beginning to pay dividends: Lome is the site of West Africa's first private offshore bank, which will finance regional projects. And in January 1987, for the first time in several years, the Togo government was not forced to reschedule debts.

Kenya's Task Force on Privatization has for the past three years been examining the disposal of some of the country's more than 400 enterprises in which the government has an interest. Progress has been delayed because of political reservations about selling enterprises to the only available buyers — particular ethnic groups or foreign multinationals.

More promising prospects for Africa's immediate future appear to lie in leasing and management contracting of state-owned firms, which would avoid political accusations of loss of control. Leasing hotel operations has become common, as in the cases of Niger and Tanzania.

Conclusion

The developing world is rapidly becoming more sophisticated in the uses of privatization, finding ways to alleviate the political concerns that inevitably go with reducing the role of the state in the economy. Organized labor's concerns that privatization will mean loss of jobs are being met, and there is a wider public acceptance of the advantages of divestment. While the process is slow and often frustrating, it is becoming clear that in many countries the private sector can replace inefficient, money-losing state enterprises with more modern industrial plants that will better serve the needs of the consumer as well as relieve financial pressures on the government.

3

M. Peter McPherson

The Promise of Privatization

Every so often I come across a list of ideas that someone believes are changing the world. My list would certainly include privatization. The idea of turning over government-owned enterprises to the private sector is sweeping — and changing — the developing world.

This publication is the result of an international conference on privatization sponsored by the United States Agency for International Development (USAID), held in Washington, D.C., in February 1986. The conference was significant in three respects. First, it drew nearly five hundred delegates from forty-six countries. Never before had so many decision-makers and technical authorities from so many countries been brought together in one place to discuss, to deliberate, and finally, to act on privatization. Second, the conference was a dramatic celebration of change. Secretary of State George P. Shultz underlined this point when he told delegates that the conference symbolized a "revolution in economic thinking. It has been an unusual revolution," the Secretary explained, "in that it is a return to principles we once adhered to, but from which we had strayed. They are principles of individual freedom and private enterprise that have changed the world more in 200 years than all the changes in the preceding 2,000 years." Finally, the conference was more than an intellectual exercise. Agendas promoting privatization were set that are now being carried out around the world.

Privatization has finally come into the development mainstream as a result of a gradual but profound shift in attitudes worldwide concerning the beneficial role of the free market and the private sector. This shift is based on the experience of the Third World itself. Developing countries that rely on market forces as an engine for their economic systems have, by and large, grown more rapidly than those with economies that are planned, directed, and controlled by the state. Market economies have greater diversity and resilience than controlled economies. Many countries have found that state-owned enterprises have failed to generate high rates of economic growth that are critical to development. Third World leaders have, in large measure, accepted the evidence of this experience and are beginning to draw on its lessons to chart new paths toward greater economic performance for their own countries.

Privatization is at the core of this continuing dialogue. Privatization increases the quality of goods and services available in the market while keeping it responsive to consumer needs and demands. It allows governments to reduce their deficits by ending the costly subsidies they pay to keep inefficient parastatals afloat. Through the free market's allocation of resources, privatization over the long term creates more jobs and opportunities for all. Privatization leads to open, competitive economies that produce higher incomes and more permanent jobs. In short, privatization can be the right step at the right time to liberate the economies of developing countries from the slow growth or stagnation that has plagued so many of them for so long.

We can draw some broad conclusions from privatization efforts to date. First, privatization moves forward more rapidly when leaders of developing nations make highly visible political commitments to economic reform. Second, privatization does not come easily. Divestiture of state enterprises may run counter to the interests of powerful elements within a society; many state-owned enterprises are not economically or financially viable enough to attract investors; and a fear of foreign investors often permeates governments and parastatals, rendering some elements of privatization suspect. Third, there is no single model for achieving success. Privatization can range from outright sale to a private-sector buyer to the transfer of shares to employees. Although there is no ideal model that fits all situations, the prospects for privatization are greatest in countries that have financial mechanisms that facilitate privatization.

Fourth, even highly developed nations are still experimenting with privatization. Britain is in the midst of a full-scale privatization program. Forty percent of its state sector has been handed over to private enterprise in the past eight years. Yet debate about privatization continues, not just in Britain, but in Italy, Spain, and elsewhere in Europe. Nor is the United States a fully divested nation, though it is getting there. Public land is being auctioned, loan portfolios are being broken up, even our post offices are being placed in the hands of the private sector. Debates surround our government's divestiture as well. Finally, privatization is more than a matter of converting factories or public services to the private sector. It also means freeing the market of impediments, such as price controls on farmers or interest rate ceilings on lenders and borrowers. All too often, these controls have resulted in poverty and the diversion of resources away from private enterprise — factors which have radically limited economic growth in developing nations. In other words, privatization cannot be carried out in a vacuum. Macroeconomic policies such as extending credit to private borrowers, developing capital market structures, and reducing government regulation are essential to successful privatization.

The United States Agency for International Development has taken a leading role in responding to this worldwide interest in privatization. We have made privatization a significant component of our Private Enterprise Initiative, whose goal is to build a favorable climate for free enterprise in the developing world. A significant financial and technological commitment has been made to help developing countries privatize their economies. USAID will continue to promote macroeconomic reforms that encourage growth based on market forces. We will continue to make privatization a major element of our policy dialogue with host country governments. The United States will continue to work with the international financial community to view privatization as a worthwide investment for future economic growth. As a result of the conference, USAID has directed Agency missions in forty countries to carry out an average of two privatization activities annually. Working with the Departments of Treasury and State, USAID will continue to encourage multilateral development banks to act more decisively in private-sector lending, privatization, and divestiture.

The development approaches of the past, based on large government bureaucracies and centralized, government-controlled economies, have been discredited by their failure. Privatization is forging economic success and stability. Privatization works because it focuses on the entrepreneur, encourages individual initiative, and promotes market-oriented policies. More and more developing countries are discovering that privatization produces growth for their economies and greater opportunities for a broader spectrum of their people.

Part II

The Foundations of Privatization

4

Elliot Berg

The Role of Divestiture in Economic Growth

Privatization is a response to the rapid growth of government in the last twenty years. International Monetary Fund (IMF) figures show that from 1960 to 1980 the public expenditures of most countries rose by 2 to 3 percent a year in real terms, especially from 1960 to 1975. In the early 1970s, thirteen countries were spending close to 30 percent of their GNP in the public sector; by the end of the decade about forty countries — almost half the ninety countries for which the IMF keeps statistics — were spending more than a third of their GNP in the public sector. A kind of quiet revolution occurred in the 1970s, shifting resources into the public sector. In less-developed countries (LDCs), the growth of the public sector was characterized by growth of the parastatal sector, the state-owned enterprises (SOEs). The numbers are revealing:

- In Mexico, 150 SOEs existed at the beginning of the 1960s; by 1980 that figure had reached at least 400, and there is now talk of 600 SOEs;

- In Brazil, there were 150 SOEs at the beginning of the 1960s; by the beginning of the 1980s there were 600 to 700; and

- In Tanzania, there were fifty SOEs in the mid-1960s; by the late 1970s there were 400.

State-owned enterprises now account for 10 to 20 percent of GNP in much of the less-developed world. They dominate manufacturing in a great number of countries. In Turkey, for example, 50 percent of value added is generated by state-owned manufacturing enterprises. The figure is 80 percent in Egypt, and in very few poorer countries is it less than 30 or 40 percent. The same is true of capital investment. SOEs are now responsible for between 20 and 60 percent of total investment spending in the less-developed world. This trend cuts across ideologies and types of economic systems. Whether in Kenya, the Ivory Coast, or Brazil, the same propensities exist for expansion of the state sector. This is true of the statist, socialist economies as well; virtually all countries saw an expansion of the public sector and SOEs in the 1960s and 1970s.

This increase in the size of the state has become a great problem, especially for a certain group of economies for which there are not many sources of growth. Theorists and politicians claimed SOEs were the leading edge of modernization, especially in manufacturing. SOEs were to generate resources for investment and take control away from foreign interests, which were resented in much of the world. The perception now, of course, is that these SOEs on which so much hope was placed have failed. SOEs are seen more as budget drains than generators of new resources. Governments everywhere are searching for new ways to mobilize resources and use the resources they have more effectively, and this has fueled the shift to the private sector.

The push for privatization comes in different forms in different parts of the world. In the industrial countries, it has come mainly through divestiture—through privatization of ownership and sale of equity. In the socialist and centrally planned economies, it has come—to the extent that it has come at all—in the individualization of economic activity. The most striking example, of course, is China, but the trend can also be seen in Hungary and other centrally planned economies.

In the LDCs, there is a mixture of approaches. Some divestiture has been accomplished in the fashion of the industrial countries. Singapore Airlines sold a substantial share of its equity on private markets. Malaysia is privatizing a major port facility. And the telecommunications systems of several Southeast Asian countries are being privatized by sale of stock to the public. But in most of the less-developed world, divestiture remains a rare event. There are extremely few cases of privatization of the kind that can be found in the industrialized countries — the sale of equity. What is more common is reprivatization, particularly in the two champion performers, Bangladesh and Chile. A similar phenomenon can be found in both these cases: when a traumatic war in Bangladesh split the country, those who owned enterprises in what is now Bangladesh fled, leaving the state to take control of those enterprises; in Chile a spasm of political revolution resulted in roughly 500 enterprises being taken over in one form or another during the three-year period of Allende's rule in the early 1970s.

Problems of Privatization

A few years ago I did a study that tried to determine exactly what was happening with divestiture of SOEs around the world. After looking through all the literature and talking to anybody who knew anything, we found only thirty actual divestitures in Africa, about 165 in Latin America, and around 250 in Asia in the last decade. If Bangladesh and Chile are eliminated from these figures, we find only 100 or so divestitures around the world. The question thus arises: Why has there been so little divestiture in the LDCs compared with the industrialized countries? After all, if you pick up any newspaper in Western Europe you will find two or three articles about the sale of state enterprises by Italy, Sweden, Germany, Japan, and, of course, the champion industrial privatizer, the United Kingdom. Yet little of the same has occurred in the LDCs.

I think this is in part because of the novelty of the phenomenon. But there are other factors at work, of which I will mention three. First, the motivation for divestiture is very different in industrial countries compared with most LDCs. In the industrialized countries, privatization involves a search for more dynamic management. There are other motives, but the basic thrust is to invigorate the management of important companies—many of which are vital to the health of the nations' economies—so that they may perform better. A few LDCs want to stimulate better management through privatizing, but the main objective is to get rid of losers. These governments are burdened with a whole array of state enterprises that obviously do not function well and are drains on budget and credit resources. Privatization—or more properly, divestiture—is seen as a way to reduce these fiscal and monetary burdens.

The second difference has to do with the availability of modalities of privatization or divestiture. In the industrial countries, the question of selling stock is essentially financial: once the political decision is made, the rest can proceed smoothly. The process involves finding the right merchant bankers, getting the right valuation of assets, then finding a good price and putting the company up for sale, usually in a well-developed capital market. Divestitures can even take the form of widespread management buyouts of SOEs. In the LDCs, this road is not as readily available, for well-known reasons. The matter of who buys state assets is largely irrelevant in industrialized countries; in the LDCs it is of overwhelming importance. LDCs have thin capital markets with few potential buyers for state enterprises. In many countries, foreigners are not regarded as acceptable buyers for political and social reasons. Some countries have ethnic restrictions as well, and there is great reluctance to undertake privatization or divestiture programs because "undesirables" may buy the companies.

The third factor—not unrelated, of course—is that the economic policy environment in the two sets of countries is very different. In the industrialized countries, a state enterprise that migrates into the private sector finds a well-structured legal system, a reasonably competitive market without excessive controls over prices and inputs, and a relatively open international trading structure. The typical LDC, in contrast, has a legal structure intolerant of private activity, labor laws that are extremely restrictive in terms of who can be hired and fired, total or nearly total protectionism in the industrial sector, subsidized access to credit resources, and a government that fixes wage and price levels. This economic structure is a different kind of animal from that of industrial countries, and it creates special problems.

Further Difficulties

Let us further explore difficulties of divestiture in the less-developed world. The first I have already mentioned: most governments are primarily anxious to get rid of losers—firms that are not making any profits, may never be able to make profits, and are drains on public resources and management skills. Second, there is the limited number of capital-bearing buyers. Third, in small economies, many governments see little advantage in transferring a public sector monopoly to the private sector, where it could become a private sector monopoly. In fact, this is the case for the manufacturing sector in most of the small economies of the world.

Fourth, it is important to note that the domestic political constituency for privatization—and especially for divestiture—is small in many LDCs. If you look at who is for and against divestiture, you will find that intellectuals in virtually all of the developing world are against it. They see it as selling off national assets to the power brokers, which they think is a terrible idea. The military is often opposed to privatization in places like Turkey, Brazil, and Argentina, where it initiated many of the SOEs. In some countries, half of the industrial sector is run by the ministry of defense, which will certainly be against privatization. Labor, whether formally or informally organized, is against it mainly because overmanning is a problem inherent in all state sectors, and reduction in staff is a consequence of divestiture. Bureaucrats are against it, again for obvious reasons: they don't want to see their particular interests shrink away. In short, one must look hard and long to find a constituency for a divestiture program. And that's part of the problem, because so far the major forces for privatization have been outsiders—the World Bank and the IMF.

Finally, it is only fair to mention that the political risks to any leadership that heads down this road are extremely high. The process of divestiture involves an admission of national guilt, as it were: the great number of white elephants constituting huge deficits means that terrible mistakes were made. Divestiture is a very tough political action to take, and very few governments have shown themselves willing to take it. A story illustrates just how difficult this can be. A methanol/gasohol plant built in Kenya cost a billion Kenyan shillings. It never operated, and the best offer for the plant was 5 million shillings. To accept such a price for this huge piece of machinery and publicly admit that it was a gross failure would have been extremely difficult. And the government, of course, never did.

Despite the difficulties, privatizations *are* occurring. In addition, there are many internal divestitures taking place: firms or enterprises are shedding activities that are the least profitable (or the most money-losing). For example, the Ivory Coast had twelve rice mills in the state sector that were not particularly viable. Of these, half were closed and half were leased to private companies. In Panama, several nonviable sugar complexes were closed. And in other countries, many airlines — which are big money-losers — have abandoned domestic routes or released aircraft to international carriers. Pruning costs has reduced the burdens of the enterprises.

This type of internal divestiture removes state-owned monopolies from the market, creating the potential for private initiative. Some enterprises are simply closing their doors and wasting away. Budget resources and access to credit at central or commercial banks are cut, and people are laid off gradually over a year or two. Under the pressure of fiscal and monetary austerity, governments are forced to make decisions about which enterprises will survive, and many of them are closing. In Turkey, for example, one of the granddaddies of all SOEs has been greatly pruned simply by credit neglect and deregulation. The Meat and Fish Corporation, which only six or seven years ago employed perhaps 250,000 people, has now shrunk to about 100,000. There is vibrant competition from private slaughterhouses, which was never the case until now.

Finally, there is "back-door privatizing." In Madagascar, for example, there appears to be little private sector development. But when you begin talking to people, you find that decentralized, unpublicized shifting of emphasis from the state to the private sector is taking place. Hotels are being leased to private management. Returning to one hotel where

I had been before, I was astonished to see how much the service had improved. I asked what had happened and was told that it had been leased to a Mauritian family at a flat rate. The change was amazing, but not a word was spoken about privatization.

The Importance of Knowledge

First, even the most casual survey suggests that for successful privatization, much more must be known about individual enterprises than is typically known. Any divestiture program based on a vague understanding of the enterprises in question will surely run into serious problems. Often, failing enterprises won't have annual accounts for the previous three or four years. Authoritative studies of SOEs that we consider to be nonviable are needed to convince people of the desirability of a particular action. These studies should define and classify the enterprise. If an enterprise will never succeed, it should be liquidated. Enterprises that the government considers strategic, or those that the government will not even *consider* turning over to the private sector should be rehabilitated. There are some enterprises for which partial privatization may be right, and for these, 30 percent of the equity might be sold. For others, total privatization may be the answer. Very few such studies exist, and we often enter into divestment negotiations not knowing enough about the nature of the enterprises and their potential.

Second, we need more openness in negotiations despite its disadvantages; there is great risk with closed-door dealing. In many countries, the people sitting around the table at a divestiture or privatization discussion may also be actors in the purchase. A minister of finance may have an interest with others in buying the enterprise in question. There is always the danger of such things happening. Finally, the benefits of divestiture must be stressed. Much discussion of divestiture and of privatization in general tends to be negative, with great emphasis on reduction in employment and the scaling down or liquidation of national assets. There is little public discussion of the benefits of better resource use, reduction of pressures on the budget, and the reallocation of labor — and management in particular — to more productive tasks.

So far I have discussed the privatization of ownership, but that is only one form of privatization. I think it is probably the least amenable to rapid change, for the reasons given above. In many circumstances it may be as important to change the regulatory environment. Clearly, in the case of an urban bus system, where passenger lines are heavily subsidized by the state, a change to private ownership is not going to matter much so long as the rate structure is rigidly controlled. Deregulation is necessary to allow effective competition. Another possibility, one that may not be so easy for some of us to swallow, is that divestiture may not be a desirable solution for certain enterprises. The company may have a heritage of poor decisions, or there may have been technological changes in the world economy such that divestiture may not be viable. In those cases, the discussion should be focused on whether or not to liquidate.

What, then, are the most promising sectors to approach for quick results? First, there is the privatization of management. We know that leasing provides a politically acceptable foot in the door; this is probably the best way to begin, since by various arrangements on the leasing side the degree of write-down of assets can be controlled. We found relatively few examples of leasing, but the approach has a lot going for it. With the use of contracting out, it clearly has immense potential. Road maintenance is a critical sector in many countries, and urban services—waste collection and so on—is another area with tremendous potential. Not much has been done in this area, although Caracas now has its streets cleaned by a private company. Finally, there is general deregulation of the economy. Even in economies that are at early stages of development, a great deal can be done in transportation, agricultural marketing, education and health, and animal services. In key sectors of the poorest countries, where the state now has a monopoly on the delivery of services to producers, there is immense potential for privatization.

In short, while privatizations of ownership have been few so far, privatization of management as well as load shedding via deregulation or contracting out are promising and suitable for economies at all stages of development. It may be more promising to pursue deregulation and the privatization of management. The forces of austerity in LDCs are working toward deregulation, and we should promote these avenues of privatization. For the past twenty-five years, the tremendous energies of individuals and small groups have been neglected or suppressed by the size of the state; there is great potential waiting to be unlocked. Deregulation and privatization are the keys to renewing economic growth in the world.

5

Robert Poole

The Political Obstacles
to Privatization

Privatization in industrialized countries is far more extensive than is generally realized. While much international attention has been focused on the transfer of major national enterprises such as the British and Japanese national railways, the actual number of these examples is rather small. On the other hand, tens of thousands of less dramatic, smaller-scale cases of privatization exist at the state and local levels in the United States, Great Britain, West Germany, and Japan.

In this paper, I concentrate on various forms of privatization of public service delivery systems rather than the large-scale divestiture of state-owned enterprises (SOEs). I believe the former are the best initial prospects for privatization and for demonstrating that privatization can provide meaningful improvements in a country's economy. Privatization of services may set a precedent for looking at the phenomenon itself, and for making it more politically acceptable for larger-scale enterprises that may be more difficult to tackle.

Numerous obstacles remain to the spread of privatization. Among them are simple misconceptions, which those who favor maintaining the status quo promote as if they were truths.

Misconceptions about Privatization

"There won't be enough suppliers to permit competition." The implication of this claim is that only one of a handful of firms will actually be qualified or willing to enter a field, leading to a monopolistic or oligopolistic situation that will harm consumers; hence the status quo of state provision should be maintained.

The first problem with this view is the assumption that a permanent public monopoly is better than a temporary private monopoly. Numerous studies of how bureaucracies actually perform dispel the naive notion that civil servants are any more altruistic or enlightened, on the average, than entrepreneurs. And because a public monopoly is generally permanent, consumers have no hope of an alternative if its service is costly or of low quality. Turning the service over to one or a few private firms under conditions that permit competition at least offers consumers the chance of improvements, as new suppliers are ultimately attracted by the monopoly profits being earned by the initial entrant.

But the reality is likely to be even better for consumers. In virtually every field of public service, many possible suppliers exist. For example:

- The employees of a public service agency can form a company and bid for the contract to provide the service;
- Administrators frustrated by bureaucratic constraints will often be motivated to form companies to do the same work more efficiently;
- Firms in related fields may be attracted by the chance to diversify into a new area;
- Many labor-intensive public services are ideal start-up businesses for lone entrepreneurs, of which there will always be a good supply if the opportunity to make money is present (gar-

bage collection, jitneys, landscape maintenance, and janitorial services are a few examples).

"Many public services are natural monopolies, so they should be operated by the public sector." There are two relevant questions to ask about this assertion. First, are the services in question really natural monopolies? And second, even if they are, is public ownership best?

All too often, existing providers of a service claim that their field is naturally monopolistic or oligopolistic in order to prevent the introduction of competition. For decades this claim supported public utility–type regulation of airlines, railroads, bus lines, trucking, and taxicab service in the United States. But within the past decade significant deregulation has occurred in all of these areas, leading to expanded service and lower average prices for the great majority of consumers. Even such traditional public utilities as telecommunications are being opened up to competition, and studies of even limited competition among both electricity firms and cable TV firms show lower costs and greater responsiveness to consumers. We should be very suspicious of claims that a given public service represents a natural monopoly, and we certainly should not protect any provider against entry by other would-be providers.

Even where there is a political consensus that a utility should be provided through a monopoly, it is not at all clear that state ownership is the preferred form. American telephone service has generally been acknowledged to be among the cheapest and best in the world. Yet it has always been provided by private — though regulated — franchised monopolies. Most U.S. electricity and most French water supply systems are also provided by private enterprise. I contend that the *possibility* of competition in the private sector is a better protection for consumers than the *guaranteed* monopoly of a public sector bureaucracy, given what we have learned about the relative performance of the public sector versus the private sector in terms of both cost and responsiveness.

"The service must be provided by the state to ensure that the poor will have access to it." This widely believed proposition is a major reason why so many public services are provided by the state and made available without charge to users, often at heavily subsidized prices.

Ironically, such policies can actually be harmful to the poor. A heavily subsidized transit system, for example, does manage to keep its prices low. But there are numerous other consequences of subsidization: a lack of cost consciousness by management and employees; continuation of little-used routes and toleration of above-market pay scales and inefficient work policies, for instance. The result is often a very costly transit system that is not responsive to changing demands for service. The poor are especially vulnerable because they rely heavily on public transit. Moreover, although the poor receive the greatest benefit from subsidized prices, they themselves pay many of the taxes used to provide the subsidies through sales or value-added taxes, property taxes (as part of their rent), and corporate taxes (as part of product prices). There is also the huge waste involved in subsidizing the majority of riders, who are not poor and who could readily afford to pay market rates.

A far more efficient alternative is to make use of what the U.S. Department of Transportation calls user-side subsidies, which entails subsidizing only those users who are too poor to pay market-level prices, and letting everyone else pay the full rate. The transit system can then be run as a business, presumably by private entrepreneurs interested in getting the job done in the most efficient way. This mechanism is usually accomplished through vouchers. The state can issue transit vouchers, health care vouchers, housing vouchers, or school vouchers, each redeemable only for the designated service, that the service provider can present for reimbursement by the state. The provision of vouchers solves the problem of access by the poor, allowing facilities to open up entire areas to more efficient provision of services by private enterprise.

"Public services should be organized for service, not profit." This objection is purely emotional or ideological, with little real application to reality. Even the most sensitive of services—whether it be the skill of a surgeon or the compassion of a clergyman—are rewarded with a regular income. Everyone (other than those who take a vow of poverty and live as ascetics) engages in a trade or profession in order to "profit." What separates productive economies from stagnating ones is the presence or absence of human motivation to devote talents most

effectively toward identifying and meeting the real needs of others. This is precisely what entrepreneurship is designed to do. By ruling some areas of life off limits to entrepreneurship, a society denies itself a vital source of innovation and creativity. The desire for profit is what motivates entrepreneurs to seek out and fill the vast diversity of human needs. There is no dichotomy between profit and public service.

Each of the foregoing misconceptions can serve the interests of those opposed to privatization, whether they be a bureaucracy unwilling to shift its role from service provider to that of contract administrator, or the franchised monopolist desperately fighting to prevent the introduction of competing firms. In each case, however, both theory and evidence can be used to discredit these propositions.

Real Barriers to Privatization

While it is important to dispel misconceptions such as those discussed above, it is also necessary to recognize that there are a number of very real barriers to privatization that, unless dealt with, can restrict or prevent services from being shifted from public to private operation. Five of the barriers discussed below are frequently encountered at the state and local levels in the United States, and are likely to arise elsewhere as well. The sixth is more likely to be a problem unique to developing countries.

Misleading cost accounting. Claims that private enterprise can deliver a service at less cost are often met with counterclaims by current state providers. Unfortunately, the costs of state service provision are often greatly understated, by any of the following means:

- Quoting price as if it were cost. Some city officials have compared the proposed price to be charged by a would-be private supplier with the price charged by the government agency, ignoring the fact that the firm must price to cover all of its costs while the government is generally subsidized.

- Ignoring overhead costs. If a city government got out of the garbage collection business, for example, a portion of the city's general overhead costs would no longer exist. It is necessary to include the garbage collection department's share of city overhead in order to make a fair comparison. But this is often not done.

- Ignoring retirement costs. Many U.S. cities operate a retirement system for all city departments. Generally, these costs do not show up in each department's budget, yet they are very real and large costs of operating that department.
- Ignoring capital costs. Most governments do not include the costs of buying major pieces of equipment (such as vehicles or heavy machinery) in departmental operating budgets. Hence, unlike commercial firms, no annual depreciation charges are made to account for the eventual replacement of these assets.
- Inaccurate or incomplete accounting. The lack of audited financial statements presents a major obstacle to comparing the costs of a public enterprise with what the costs would be under private enterprises.

Properly accounting for all of these factors will give a realistic picture of the true costs of public and private provision of the service in question. One must never rely on the department whose continued existence is in question to produce such a comparison. It is essential that a knowledgeable but disinterested external party (a public accounting firm, for instance) perform these important cost comparisons.

Fear of job losses and unemployment. One reason privatization frequently lowers costs is that public sector enterprises tend to be overstaffed. All too often, agency or department heads see their task as providing employment rather than delivering the particular service in the most cost-efficient manner. This naturally leads to protective work policies such as restrictions on the use of part-time labor and arbitrary division of work in departments as well as simply hiring more people than are needed to do the job.

This policy rests on a mistaken notion of the role of work in society. It does not serve a country's economy to waste resources. If ten people are employed for a task that can be done by six, the other four are unavailable for productive work elsewhere, and the funds absorbed in paying them are unavailable to pay them for productive work. If people are paid a salary in a public bureaucracy to do work that doesn't need to be done, it is depriving the rest of society of the skills and services of those people. In the short term, this policy gives those people jobs, but in the long term it prevents them from doing productive work in other fields. Employment should not be substituted for efficiency as a principal management objective.

Nevertheless, when the transition from public to private is proposed, the fear of creating at least short-term unemployment can pose a significant political barrier. It is therefore important to develop techniques for dealing with this problem. Among the methods used in American cities and counties are the following:

- Contractor preference requirements. When a service is first being privatized, the state can require that the company or companies taking over give first preference in hiring to the displaced government workers.

- Phased-in privatization. Another option is to implement privatization gradually, usually on a geographical district basis. Public employees displaced by the first privatization can be transferred to other (not yet privatized) districts to fill any vacancies arising from normal attrition (turnover in state and local public services can range from as little as 5 percent to as much as 20 percent per year).

- Worker enterprises. Government employees in an enterprise slated for privatization should always be given the option of forming a company and bidding for the contract in competition with the other bidders. A variant of this idea is to require a department to bid against outside firms without requiring conversion to corporate status. If the department wins the bidding, it continues to perform the function in accordance with the terms of its bid (which may mean a significant revision of work policies and fewer total employees). If it loses, the work goes to the winning outside firm, which may or may not offer to hire the now displaced workers.

Finally, wherever possible, it is wise to give affected parties a stake in privatization. The compensation of agency administrators can be based on achievement of the maximum level of performance per unit of money spent instead of on the size of the agency (as measured in money and numbers of employees). This gives the administration a tangible incentive to seek out more cost-effective ways to operate, such as contracting out. Similarly, when a state agency is denationalized, the natural fear and opposition of the work force may be overcome if it is given (or allowed to purchase cheaply) shares of stock in the newly privatized company. This method has been used with great success in Britain.

One example of a public-to-private transition involved the contracting out of data processing services in Orange County, California. Orange County is the second-largest county in California; a very large department did all of the data processing for the county government. A number of firms offered bids for a seven-year contract, and the winning firm's bid amounted to something like a 25 percent reduction in the annual cost compared with the county's estimate. In addition, the winning firm offered jobs to virtually all of the existing employees. Clearly, the firm would have a problem if it intended to keep all of the employees but charge the county only 75 percent of the previous price. It needed to reduce the level of employment within the first few years in order to meet the contract and not go broke. The firm succeeded, using two methods.

One was to offer lateral transfers to other parts of the firm, once it became familiar with the new employees. The firm happened to be the Computer Sciences Corporation, a fairly large provider of computer services in the United States, so there were many job openings throughout the company's operation. The other method was simply to take advantage of normal employment turnover, somewhere between 5 and 10 percent per year. For the first several years, vacant positions were not filled, and work was reorganized and functions absorbed. Utilizing mainly these two methods, the company was able to cut the work force by about 20 percent in the first two years of the contract and succeed in meeting the bid price to the county.

The firm was also successful in motivating the employees to work for it, first because the firm had a good reputation in the computer field, and second because the possibility of transfers to other parts of the company opened up career paths to employees that they would not have had working for the county government. The trade-off was the security of civil service employment for opportunities to do more interesting and different types of work within the company.

Fear of corruption. One ever-present danger with the contracting-out form of privatization is that one bidder will make an under-the-table deal with the contracting agency whereby it is awarded the contract in exchange for illegal considerations. Such instances have occurred in American cities and counties—though they appear to be the exception rather than the rule. Opponents of privatization take great pains to publicize such events, hoping to discredit the entire phenomenon based on a small number of examples.

The solution is to have clear-cut, open bidding procedures and written, objective selection criteria and to make sure they are followed. This can be done by requiring that such rules, procedures, and criteria be matters of public record and by holding bid openings and other important decision-making sessions in public. Several detailed handbooks on methods to be used in contracting have been published during the past several years, compiling lessons from the experience of thousands of local governments in the United States.

The problem of corruption is much less serious when privatization takes the form of "load shedding," whereby the state simply decides to cease provision of a particular service in favor of leaving it to the marketplace. When individuals are free to select their own providers (as is the case with bus service in Buenos Aires, for example), then it is the granting or withholding of their patronage that determines whether a particular firm grows, shrinks, or remains in business at all. The only way a firm can use bribery to increase its share of business in a competitive marketplace is to "bribe" potential customers with lower prices or better service.

Legal prohibitions. Explicit legal restrictions stating that government itself must perform a particular service can be another significant barrier to privatization. In some cases the administrative law may be ambiguous or unclear, leading cautious interpreters to conclude that the service may not be delegated to the private sector, while other interpreters conclude the opposite. In order for privatization to be possible in these cases, legislative reform must be researched, drafted, and enacted.

In the United States, private sector firms wishing to enter a particular field are frequently the ones to take on the task of developing legislative or administrative provisions to remove barriers to privatization. In a number of states private firms are attempting to get permits to build and/or operate prisons. Most state laws do not permit the state to delegate its correctional power to commercial enterprises, but where such provisions have been modified, companies headed by experienced correctional people have begun to operate. In some cases they have bid on and been awarded contracts to operate existing jails or prisons. A more recent development is the turnkey contract, under which the firm raises funds, designs, and builds the correctional facility, then operates it under long-term contract.

Although the impetus for removing legal barriers often comes from private sector entities, enlightened public sector officials in both England and the United States have sometimes made the removal of legal barriers a priority in the interest of greater efficiency in government. They have come to see that making lower-cost, more responsive public services possible via privatization and/or deregulation can be a politically popular move. Although they risk loss of favor with status quo interests (public employees, franchised private firms), they stand to gain popularity with taxpayers and private enterprise service providers. Deregulation of airlines and trucking was a popular pro-consumer issue for liberal Democratic senator Edward M. Kennedy in the United States. Privatization has become a popular pro-taxpayer issue for Prime Minister Margaret Thatcher in Britain. A particularly good time to introduce privatization proposals is during elections.

Regulatory problems. Another potential obstacle to privatization is an adverse climate of government regulation. Municipal bus systems in the United States were once almost entirely private enterprises. But most local governments, operating on the mistaken notion that bus service is a natural monopoly, imposed stringent price controls and service requirements on the bus companies. When Americans moved to the suburbs in massive numbers following World War II, the companies were severely restricted from being able to adapt to the changed patterns of settlement and transportation. It became far more costly to serve a dispersed, low-density population, but political pressures from riders prevented adequate fare increases. Numerous routes became unprofitable, but political pressures caused them to be maintained. One after another, the bus companies went bankrupt and were taken over by the local governments.

Today transit economists are advocating a competitive model for urban transit rather than the old public utility model. In this case the developed world can learn many lessons from the cities of the developing world, where competition with state-owned transit is commonly permitted (Calcutta, Caracas, Dakar, Manila, and Singapore are a few examples). In some cases private enterprise provides virtually all bus and taxi systems, as in Buenos Aires and Hong Kong. But if private transit entrepreneurs are encouraged to enter the business, it would be a profound mistake to resurrect price controls and service requirements, since these might lead to yet another wave of bankruptcies. Public officials need to understand that competition is an *alternative* to state-imposed regulation and price controls, and should give the providers incentives for responsive behavior.

Regulation of prices may well be needed if there is only one supplier in the marketplace, but when there are multiple suppliers, there is no need for price controls. In fact, in a great many LDCs, and in Britain and the United States as well, private enterprise has been driven out of certain fields by the existence and persistence of price controls. Transit is a particularly good example: where transit in American cities used to be provided entirely by private enterprise, price controls have been exerted as part of their exclusively franchised monopolies. Over a period of years, political pressure always led to holding the prices below levels that were necessary for the companies to survive, so the companies went bankrupt. State and local governments took over these companies, and that led to subsidized operation, which has now produced very costly and ineffective transit systems. It would be a great mistake to privatize but leave price controls intact: it would prescribe that the same situation happen again.

Likewise, in denationalizing large-scale SOEs that have functioned as statutory monopolies, it is important that public policy-makers also open the way for competition. The Thatcher administration has been criticized for allowing only a single competitor to the newly privatized British Telecom (and only in a limited segment of BT's business, that

of commercial long-distance service). Consumers would have been better served by complete legalization of entry into all aspects of the telephone business, as is occurring in the United States.

Inadequate legal structures. Privatization depends upon the willingness of entrepreneurs to risk their own funds toward developing an
enterprise in the hope that it will meet the needs of enough customers
to cover the entrepreneur's costs. But the willingness of entrepreneurs
and those who lend them money to take those risks depends very much
on the legal environment in which they seek to operate. If the law does
not contain strong protection for private ownership of property and
for the sanctity of contracts, backed by an impartial, smoothly working judicial system, then entrepreneurship is unlikely to develop and
flourish. What entrepreneurial energies remain will likely be channeled
into the underground or informal economy instead. In many countries,
both developed (like Italy) and less developed (like Peru), thriving informal sectors testify to the gross inadequacy of one or more key elements
of the legal system. It is crucial to institute better access to courts, stronger legal protections, and a tax code that does not penalize investment
and allows people to have a realistic chance of making money from
being entreprenuers and investing in public services. Privatization, in
fact, can provide the impetus for these reforms.

Lack of financing. One of the major barriers to privatization is
the lack of financing by international lending agencies and the international banks, many of whom, it seems, would rather collect payments
from a government than risk their money on entrepreneurs. In countries that do not have well-developed financial markets, virtually the
only sources of funding are those agencies. Fortunately, this situation
is changing. Participation of representatives of the World Bank and the
Asian and African development banks in privatization conferences and
other activities indicates that a significant shift of emphasis on the part
of international lending agencies may be taking place. They have been
hurt badly over the last decade by the extent to which their loans to
SOEs have turned bad or remained unpaid. A serious rethinking about
the different performance incentives of SOEs versus private firms may
be taking place. On average, a good private firm may be a better risk,
due to the nature of the incentives that govern its performance, than
an SOE.

Conclusion

Despite a growing body of international evidence that competition and entrepreneurship can generally provide public services more responsively and less expensively than can monopoly and bureaucracy, privatization and deregulation are still the exception rather than the rule. What stands in the way is the politics of contending interests. Defenders of the status quo can often maintain their positions by relying on misconceptions about public services and privatization as well as on some very real barriers. Overcoming these obstacles requires a new kind of leadership: the public official or political candidate who can change the calculus of interests so that citizens (as both taxpayers and service users) learn the connection between privatization/deregulation and lower costs and better service. It requires the ability to understand both the principles of good economics and the political reality of achieving them. It means figuring out the obstacles and their sources, the constituencies in favor and against, and the means to find the way around obstacles without destroying the principles. As John Redwood said about the British privatization of public housing, "We did not announce that we [were] going to sell the public housing. We announced . . . we were going to confer a right to buy the house you live in." The economic substance was the sale. But the political substance was the conferring, rather than the taking away, of a right. It is an important distinction of which consultants from the development community need to be aware.

6

Steve H. Hanke

The Necessity of
Property Rights

Over the past fifty years most governments have assumed a greater role in the economic affairs of their nations. There has been more emphasis on macroeconomic planning and management; public sector budgets have grown in absolute terms and in relation to private sector activity. This growth has been the result of rapid increases in welfare programs, military expenditures, and the range and scale of public infrastructure and services. Many countries have increased the scope of government by embracing the concept of an entrepreneurial state: a state that is allegedly the engine of growth and development, and one that attempts to achieve growth by either operating nationalized industries or intervening heavily in the operation of private firms. Finally, some countries have adopted socialist and communist economic systems — usually involuntarily — for ideological reasons.

This trend toward more government involvement in economic

affairs has begun to be seriously questioned. Indeed, there have been attempts to rely more heavily on deregulated free markets for the allocation of resources. The superiority of private enterprise is not, of course, a new idea. In 1776, Adam Smith wrote in *The Wealth of Nations* that "no two characters seem more inconsistent than those of trader and sovereign,"[1] because people are more prodigal with the wealth of others than with their own. Public administration is negligent and wasteful, he said, noting that public lands provided only 25 percent of what comparable private lands did. Consequently, Smith recommended that the remaining public commons be privatized. If this were to occur, the new owners would have the incentive to monitor activities, eliminate waste, and maximize the present value of their assets. As he put it: "The attention of the sovereign can be at best a very general and vague consideration of what is likely to contribute to the better cultivation of the greater part of his dominions. The attention of the landlord is particular and minute consideration of what is likely to be the most advantageous application of every inch of ground upon his estate."[2]

Property Rights Theory

In recent years a large corpus of analysis has been developed on the economics of property rights. This literature shows that alternative forms of property ownership give rise to different economic incentives and, subsequently, different economic results. Private enterprises are owned by individuals who are free, within the limits of the law, to use and exchange their private property rights in these assets. These rights give individual owners "residual claim" on the assets of private enterprise. When these assets are used to produce goods and services that consumers demand at costs lower than market prices, profits are generated, and the income and wealth of property owners are increased. Alternatively, if production costs exceed market prices, losses are incurred, and the value of a firm, along with the income and wealth of the owners of the firm's assets, is diminished. Stated differently, owners of private firms gain from efficient management and bear the costs of inefficient management. Private owners ultimately face the "bottom line," which measures profits (or losses) that owners claim.

Incentives created by private property rights — by the link between outcomes from using private assets and the income and wealth of the owners — have profound consequences. Private owners face incentives that make it desirable to monitor the behavior of managers and employees in their enterprises, so that consumer demands are supplied in a cost-effective way over time. As a result of being subjected to this kind of monitoring, private managers are encouraged not to shirk their responsibilities or to engage in behavior that is inconsistent with maximizing the present value of the enterprise (the owners' wealth). In other words, private property rights create incentives that promote efficient performance.

By way of contrast, public enterprises are not owned by individuals who have residual claims on the assets of these organizations. The nominal owners of public enterprises, the taxpayer-owners, cannot buy or sell these assets, so they do not have strong incentives to monitor the behavior of public managers and employees. Taxpayer-owners could capture some benefits from increased efficiency of public enterprises through tax reductions. If realized, however, these incremental benefits would be spread over many taxpayers; an individual's benefits would be small. And an individual's costs of obtaining these benefits — acquiring information, monitoring public employees, and organizing an effective political force to modify the behavior of public managers and employees — would be high. The consequences of public ownership are thus predictable. Public managers and employees allocate resources (assets) that do not belong to them. Hence they do not bear the costs of their decisions; nor do they gain from efficient behavior. Since the nominal owners of public enterprises, the taxpayers, do not have strong incentives to monitor the performance of public employees, the costs of shirking are relatively low. Public employees therefore commonly seek job-related perquisites, which increase production costs and divert attention from serving consumer demands.

Public and private enterprises are similar in that they both must plan. Public planning is, however, fundamentally different from private planning. Public plans are developed by public managers and employees who neither bear the costs of their mistakes nor legally capture benefits generated by foresight. Moreover, public plans are developed by people who do not have to answer to any owners. As long as the planning rules and procedures are followed, a public plan is considered a good plan. Private planning is quite a different story. Private plans attempt to anticipate consumer demands and production costs correctly, because the present value of the private enterprise depends on correct anticipation of demands and costs. Needless to say, private planners ultimately have to answer to the owners of private enterprises, who keep a watchful eye on the value of the enterprises that they own.

From a theoretical point of view, private enterprise, which is based on private property rights, tends to be more efficient than public enterprise. Considerable empirical evidence exists to support this conclusion. For example, the "bureaucratic rule of two" states that the cost to public enterprise of producing a quantity and quality of goods and services will be double that of private enterprise. In other words, as a rule of thumb the privatization of a public enterprise will cut costs in half.

Public Enterprises in Europe

Public enterprises in Europe provide considerable evidence to support modern property rights theory. These enterprises produce everything from pots and pans to cars and trucks. They even own hotel chains. As we would expect, these enterprises are quite different from their private counterparts. The most striking feature of nationalized enterprises is their politicization. Governments appoint the boards and top management and provide subsidies, since most nationalized companies lose money. Politicians must be consulted and approve major decisions. Government therefore determines pricing, purchasing, plant location and close-down, diversification, incentive systems, executive compensation, product development, and financial policies. Labor relations are also regulated by politicians, and contrary to popular belief they are much more stormy in nationalized than in private companies. Not surprisingly, the behavior of successful managers of nationalized enterprises resembles that of politicians rather than of businessmen.

The public ownership of nationalized enterprises and accompanying politicization lead to an interesting set of comparisons between nationalized concerns and similar private concerns. Sales per employee are lower for nationalized firms. Adjusted profits per employee are lower. Physical production per employee is lower. Taxes paid per employee are lower. Costs per dollar of sales — operating expenses plus wages — are higher. Sales per dollar of investment are lower. Profits per dollar of total assets are lower. Profits per dollar of sales are lower. Sales per employee grow at a slower rate. And, with the exception of nationalized oil companies, virtually all nationalized companies generate accounting losses. In short, evidence from Europe's public enterprises shows that property rights arrangements are not neutral, and that private enterprises are more efficient than public enterprises. Nationalized industries represent public liabilities when retained in government portfolios. Once privatized, these same entities become productive private assets. The transformation of liabilities into assets represents the power of private property rights.

7

Manuel Tanoira

Privatization as Politics

The horrors resulting from government attempts to "manage" economies, even to the point of assuming the role of producers of goods and
services within economies, are not unique to any country; neither is
the benefit that typically results from reductions of these activities. The
historical record for all countries offers a thorough and systematic lesson: to the extent that government affords *all* individuals and firms
the opportunity to produce what their counterparts elsewhere in the
world have demonstrated *can* be privately produced, the result is greater
economic efficiency, growth, and employment. The only thing diminished by acting on this lesson is poverty.[1]

Given the record of private enterprise, it might seem surprising
that "privatization" is an issue at all today. One might expect, based
on this record, that political differences would focus on alternative
means for ensuring that *all* individuals are legally afforded the opportunities of private enterprise. Of course, the disparity between this lesson
and reality is accounted for by the success of certain private firms and

individuals in attaining special privileges for themselves which no
market—but any government—can provide. The reality of most Latin
American, African, and other Third World countries is that a small
portion of their respective populations have far greater economic opportunities than do the vast majority. As a colleague of Julio Bazan, my
successor as undersecretary for privatizations in the government of Raúl
Alfonsín, said, "first we've got to privatize the private sector."[2] The
extent to which "private" enterprise has been "publicized" is most extensively detailed by Hernando de Soto's *El Otro Sendero*, which, following
its initial publication in Peru, has rapidly become a best-seller in several Latin American countries and will soon be available world-wide.[3]

The Other Path clearly shows that the countries of Latin America
are less characterized by the separation of political and economic decision making than by their merger. Mr. de Soto finds that the centrali-
zation of economic and political authority in small elites is common
in governments of both left and right. In most of these countries, the
ideology of political campaigns has less to do with the *structure* of
decision-making authority—the *institutions* of either government or
economy—than with who, among the elite, will have greater "clout"
for some period of time before the next election or *coup d'etat*. The
principal constraint upon the decisions and self-aggrandizement of both
"left" and "right" elite, whether civilian or military, is the risk of revolution, for:

> a most significant difference between a revolution and a *coup
> d'etat* is to be found in their aftermaths. The former always
> requires that a broader constituency (a greater proportion of a
> country's population) must be rewarded by the new government.
> The latter frequently involves no more than changes at the mar-
> gin; recalculations of whom among the elite must be rewarded
> how much. "New government" might be a less accurate descrip-
> tion of the change engendered by many *coup d'etats* than would
> "new occupants of governmental positions."[4]

Revolution need not be violent, at least not in the ascendance of revolu-
tionaries to positions of authority. It only requires an intense and dedicated minority (witness Allende in Chile). This fact additionally
constrains the elites of "left" and "right" in their respective countries.
Thus, amidst an abundance of violence and death in Latin America,

there have been very few violent "revolutions."

Imagine a "middle" with both "left" and "right" on one side and revolution on the other; this is a picture of political reality in most of Latin America. Thus Mr. de Soto finds a closer parallel between Latin America today and European mercantilism of the fifteenth through nineteenth centuries (attacked, incidentally, by both Adam Smith and Karl Marx) than he does with any of the contemporary systems of either East or West. His characterization of "mercantilism" is reminiscent of Lord Bauer's description of "the disastrous politicization of life in the Third World," and only raises questions about what their differences might be:

> when social and economic life is extensively politicized . . . . People divert their resources and attention from productive economic activity into other areas, such as trying to forecast political developments, placating or bribing politicians and civil servants, operating or evading controls. They are induced or forced into these activities in order either to protect themselves from the all important decisions of the rulers or, where possible, to benefit from them. This direction of people's activities and resources must damage the economic performance and development of a society, since these depend crucially on the deployment of people's human, financial and physical resources.[5]

Of course, *any* proposed change of *any* given status quo will always yield *some* who expect to lose more than they will gain from the proposed changes. It is understandable that most will work in opposition to such changes. The difference in highly politicized, mercantile societies is that "some" includes *so many* of both elites *and* non-elites. Such societies, like those with state-command systems, have a population predisposed to protection of the status quo before production.

In a mercantile society, therefore, more is required of the politics of privatization in order for it to be successful than is the case in a society in which there is a clear distinction between economic and political decision-making. In the highly politicized society, privatization should be understood *as* politics, because the merger of economic and political decision-making requires it. The question "public or private?" is more difficult to answer in a mercantile society because the question itself has less meaning.

In mercantile societies privatization might mean no more than an expansion of not-so-private enterprise, or an expansion of government by another name. This is the best reason I can offer for the perpetuation of unprofitable state-owned enterprises (SOEs) in Argentina. To the people, privatization is less likely to be seen as a means for *eliminating* the enormous subsidies received by SOEs than as a means for *transferring* the protection of the state to private (in other words, not-so-private) firms. How else can the lack of public outcry be explained in the face of continuing economic travesties?

An Unprotected Public

Protected enterprise, be it private or public, is more costly to the society that allows the protection than would otherwise be the case. Perhaps if the world provided a clear comparison between an unprotected public enterprise and its protected private counterpart, the public enterprise might be found to be more productive and profitable. But if the world provided only such a choice, I would have accepted neither President Alfonsin's invitation to serve as his undersecretary for privatization nor the invitation to write this paper.

Clearly, then, my position is *not* that eliminating government ownership is a cure-all for the development of economies and societies. I would expect a country's economy to stagnate if all of its enterprise was of the protected, not-so-private, character. Indeed, I would expect the government of such a country to justify its protection of not-so-private enterprises in terms of saving jobs, even though such "saving" of jobs is a self-fulfilling proposition that ignores the jobs lost to producers in other countries. But since such losses, of course, *will* occur, the economy will continue to stagnate, and the government will have arrived at a critical juncture. It either can genuinely privatize its supposedly private sector, or it can increasingly assume ownership of the not-so-private enterprises *because* the economy was stagnating, and, obviously, the jobs still needed to be "saved."

Looking around the world, the latter option has been the more frequent choice. Of course, I have to look no further than the end of my nose, for Argentina is among those countries which have succumbed to the worst of protected enterprise—protected public enterprise. Many state-owned corporations were, in fact, once private businesses which were failing due, at least in part to the "protection" they received. The "answer" in these cases seems to have been that if a little protection yields bankruptcies, then surely a lot of protection will generate profits.

Since 1943 when Peron came to power, Argentina has served as a textbook example of protectionism's negative effects on a political economy. Entire industries—transports, communications, energy— were "nationalized" with full monopoly status. Many other companies, in diverse sectors of the economy, were subsequently transferred to the state. If these companies can be said to save jobs, it is clearly at the expense of other jobs, for they uniformly fail to generate profits, and therefore those jobs are "saved" only because all Argentinians finance their losses. Other jobs which could have been financed by the money and credit transferred to public enterprises are thereby sacrificed in order to perpetuate employment whose cost to all Argentinians far outweighs any benefit. In short, inefficiency preempts efficiency. And the perpetuation of inefficiency prevents the discovery of efficiency and the creation of new employment.

Some examples might help. The national railroads lose about $3 million per day; maintenance is very poor and service is disastrous. The national airline loses $900,000 per day and has twice as many employees per plane as do private companies. The officials of Gas del Estado, the state-owned gas distribution company, succeeded in legally preventing private enterprise (even cooperatives of users) from installing, financing, and managing their own networks even though 25 percent of the country's gas production is vented due to a lack of facilities. Yacimientos Petroliferos Fiscales has the dubious distinction of being the only oil company in the world to lose millions of dollars per day. Today only 7 percent of Latin America's telephones are in Argentina, down from 45 percent in 1945 when the national telephone company's monopoly was established. The combined deficit of the state-owned enterprises in 1985 was equal to 2.7 percent of GNP, or 75 percent of the total budget deficit. This would have been enough to pay for more than *half* the service of the country's $50 billion external debt.

But the losses in dollars of public enterprise pale in comparison with the social and economic harm which people must endure as a consequence of this ultimate form of their "protection." When adopting a monopoly position, public enterprises pose a threat to the stability, let alone the well-being, of a society; in protecting themselves, and presumably everyone else, from competition the public is ultimately unprotected. But greater than the loss of money is the loss of respect by citizens for government itself. If democracy requires respect for governmental institutions, what are the consequences for government when a monthly "protection fee" must be paid to telephone company employees in order for telephones (installed at fees of $1,000 per home and $3,000 per business) to work regularly? Monopoly begets corruption, and it diminishes workers' prospects for useful employment. After all, when Argentinians must wait up to twenty-five years to get a telephone installed, which then does not work properly, demand obviously far exceeds supply. The response to this perfect opportunity for expanding employment? The telephone company's officials oppose letting cooperatives or other private companies install their own networks.

Cases of Privatization

In this light it should be clear that I am not optimistic about the prospects for privatization in Argentina that could do much more than expand the population of not-so-private enterprises. Nonetheless, there has been some privatization in Argentina which may contradict my skepticism. In 1951, a national enterprise known as Transportes de Buenos Aires centralized all public and private providers of public transport in the city into a single monopoly. Establishment of this monopoly was the culmination of a deprivatization process that had begun in 1936 in response to the declining utilization by passengers of the government-owned tramways and underground systems. In spite of this effort to ensure the profitability of the government systems, by 1959 they were losing $40 million a year, and in 1962, Transportes de Buenos Aires was dissolved. The system was privatized by selling the buses to the employees for a nominal amount.

Today Buenos Aires is served by hundreds of private lines, equipped with modern coaches, some worth more than $100,000. Although the fare is only 10 cents, it provides sufficient profit for the owners to replace the buses before the mandatory retirement of ten years. The government's losses were turned into gain by the creation of tax-paying, instead of tax-subsidized, businesses. And the city is no longer burdened by unsafe and obsolete vehicles devoid of passenger comforts, nor plagued by continual strikes from underpaid transportation workers, all of which only produced complaints from the public. It took only a few months after this reprivatization for the improvements to become evident.

A comparable case occurred in air transport. Though fares were fixed by the government, a private local airline (Austral) succeeded in taking away passengers from the national airline (Aerolineas Argentinas) by the only means it could: providing better service at lower cost. The government's response to this benefit to consumers was to pass a law prohibiting private companies from carrying more than 50 percent of the traffic. Adding insult to injury, the law forbade private companies from serving neighboring countries, and those routes were eventually taken over by foreign airlines, resulting in increased employment for non-Argentines, if they were fortunate enough to be unprotected by their government(s). The insult *and* the injury were too much for Austral, and the private airline bordered on bankruptcy. In order to "save jobs" that would never have required "saving" but for its own actions, the government placed Austral under state administration. Even then, Austral was losing "only" $200,000 per month, compared with monthly losses of Aerolineas Argentinas in excess of $16 million. This did not deter the secretary of transportation from proposing that the bigger money-loser absorb the other in order to establish a single state-owned airline. One of my principal accomplishments while serving as a minister to President Alfonsín was contributing to the defeat of the secretary of transportation's proposal and, with the support of the president, obtaining the decision to re-privatize Austral.

The third notable case of privatization in Argentina is that of SIAM, an industrial complex which grew over the years from making bakery machinery to making refrigerators and other household appliances, iron pipe, and even locomotives. After its founding generation had passed away, it was mismanaged into bankruptcy, with huge tax and social security debts to the government. Under a special law, the military government accepted payment of this debt in the form of the company's shares. Management authority was accorded to an Air Force

General. Under his management, obsolescent equipment and products were not addressed by reinvestment, and the corresponding decline
in the company's quality and service was matched only by its mounting losses. In order to boost sales revenue, prices were set below their
costs. Of course, this meant that no matter how much the company
sold, it could not have made a profit, and without profits it could not
correct its decline.

In the face of this, Air Force Commodore Mantel argued against
the privatization of SIAM, once claiming publicly that such action was
not needed because the company was making money. And, it appears
that it was, although at additional expense to the Argentine public.
As the general explained it to friends, the company was profiting by:
1) receiving government loans at rates below inflation, 2) delaying the
payment of sales and social security taxes, and, with the money provided
by these two tactics, 3) making loans to banks. The interest earned
from these loans actually exceeded the company's operating losses.
Whether this case characterizes the not-so-private or not-so-public, it
is clearly a candidate for *real* privatization, which finally did happen
during my brief tenure with the government. Since privatization, SIAM
has hired more workers, makes a profit—and therefore pays taxes—
and is already exporting some of its products, instead of costing Argentinians the $1 million per month it had been losing.

Lingering Skepticism

In the face of these successes, why do I remain skeptical about significant privatization in Argentina? First, I would be more encouraged
by the privatization of SIAM if it were not for the unique circumstances
wherein a new civilian government, following an extremely unpopu-
lar military regime, had an opportunity to visibly demonstrate its inde-
pendence from military control. There is a general rule that the
beneficiaries of any government program will usually succeed in per-
petuating such a program if its costs of the program are borne (in the
form of taxes) by a larger population.[6] This rule is reflected in the
phrase "tyranny of the minorities"; it allows us to understand how government programs are sustained, even if a majority of citizens do not

support them. Each beneficiary is more likely to know what, and how much, he or she is receiving from a program than is a taxpayer to know first of the program, its benefits, and beneficiaries, and second how much of total taxes paid are expended for that program.

Furthermore, even with complete knowledge, the greater the number of taxpayers financing a program, the less stake each of them has in working against the program. Beneficiaries of the program, of course, will be intense in lobbying for not only its continuation but its growth (in money, if not beneficiaries). Finally, to the extent that each taxpayer is a beneficiary of one or more programs, there is always the risk of eventually losing one's own benefits by actively opposing programs providing benefits to others. The possibility of such retaliation heightens the reluctance of taxpaying beneficiaries to engage in assertive action against programs from which they do not, themselves, benefit.

Now transportation and, especially, urban transportation confounds the operation of the general rule by bringing taxpayer-passenger beneficiaries together in close contact with one another, and requiring no more of their time than they are already spending in transit for exchanging their views about a very visible shared experience. In short, government transport, unlike any other government program, virtually creates a public forum for the elimination of government transport. In the Austral airline case, I am concerned about the decree that is planned, upon its reprivatization, whereby all growth in local traffic would go to the private line. This would not concern me so much if there were two or more private lines with equal opportunity in the market place. In present circumstances, however, the possibility of a not-so-private Austral must be envisioned. For this to be a significant case of privatization — one that counteracts the mercantile process — it must be ensured that the "protection" of Aerolineas Argentinas is not merely transferred to Austral. Again, I am skeptical because I see so little of the private, and so much of the not-so-private in Argentina.

The Politics of Privatizing

The possibilities for privatization in Argentina and most other developing countries are severely conditioned by their mercantile environments.

Privatization as accomplished in a non-mercantile society is likely to be unreplicated in a mercantile society. This does not mean that there are not lessons from elsewhere that are important in any setting, including the mercantile. Indeed, I find many things in this volume's recounting of the British experience (especially the contributions by John Redwood and Messrs. Pirie and Young) that seem essential to the success of privatization in Argentina. I simply believe that *additional* steps will be required in order for privatization to succeed in Argentina or any other mercantile society.

Nonetheless, two consistent practices of the Thatcher government's privatization program provide the fundamental *direction* for any privatization program to succeed in any society. The first of these is its commitment to broadening capital ownership among the population. This would not be so important but for its second consistent practice: increasing capital ownership *by individuals*, as opposed, say, to a worker's share of a pension fund which may own stock in various corporations. Ownership through a collectivity, such as a pension fund, cannot have the same meaning for any of its members as can individual ownership. One requires decision making—such as whether to buy one company's stock, or to sell another's—by a collectivity; each contributor to the pension fund can have little effect on the decision. Indeed, each member of a pension fund is unlikely to even know what the collectivity owns, let alone feel like an individual owner. The other allows the individual owner to gain, or lose, by his own decisions.

The difference is akin to the difference an individual can feel about occupying a unit of public housing in contrast with the feeling the same individual can have about the same unit if it is individually owned. The example is especially pertinent because one of the most significant actions of the Thatcher government of Great Britain has been the steep discounts provided to occupants of public housing for the purchase of those units from the government. As an occupant of public housing, or as one of many participants in a pension fund, there exists some right of ownership. The individual contributes to both, even if by indirect taxation, and receives some benefit from both, either now (as an occupant) or in the future (as a retiree). In either situation, however, the individual cannot legally do with either asset what he might do with an asset that he directly owned.

The desire for direct, individual ownership is illustrated by the case mentioned by Messrs. Pirie and Young, wherein the members of a particular labor union were enabled, by the privatization of their company, to purchase shares in the company at a substantial discount. In spite of the union leadership's campaign to dissuade them, 96 percent of the members who could buy shares did so. These purchasers now enjoy profits from their shares, and experience the *direct* connection between their efforts and the resulting benefits.

Such measures effect changes in attitudes, from those predisposed to protection to those which are predisposed to production. They are essential to successful privatization. But in mercantile societies, where virtually everyone shares the same predisposition to protection and is suspicious of the gains of others because someone else must pay (as usually is true in these societies), proposed "demonstrations" of privatizations which will have clearly positive results and should be relatively easy to accomplish never are because mercantilism and its predispositions pose a vicious, resistant circle.

So what positive conclusions can be reached about privatization in a mercantile society? Though tentative, the conclusions of this skeptic are that a government must be elected on the platform of privatizing decision-making. Thus open and fair elections are a prerequisite, and the focus must be on a future, not a sitting government. Honesty can only aid privatization. If people vote for it, the new government bears less risk in providing it.

But could such a campaign be devised? I believe it is possible by focusing on the truth that government as owner is no more than a sizable holding company for citizen-owners. The privatization candidates would ask of voters, "why do you need a middleman (the government) to hold *your* shares for you?" And to provide the answer, "we believe that your shares are *your* shares. We believe no one can act in your interest as well as *you*." If the privatization candidates carried through on a promise to *give* away shares of SOEs, in equal amounts, to the country's citizens, they would, at the very least, unload the government (and the same citizens) of their real burdens in subsidizing unprofitable businesses. And, if the businesses thereby privatized are also free of protection, they, and their new owners, just might turn a profit.

Is this too drastic? By what criteria? I am inclined to believe that the *whole*, not just parts, must be changed in order to effectively change the attitudes by which mercantile societies are sustained.

Part III

Planning for Privatization

8
Lance Marston

Preparing for Privatization: A Decision-Maker's Checklist

Privatization without policy, procedures, and a competent, committed staff is doomed to failure. Based on my experience over the past twenty-five years working with alternative delivery systems for public services, there are three broad phases that must be considered: preparing for privatization; implementing a privatization program and project; and monitoring and enforcing a privatization agreement and applicable laws and regulations. The preparatory phase is of extreme importance, because if done properly it sets the stage for successful privatization, which turns on four central components:

- Examination of governmental organization and staff performance (organization productivity issues);
- Selection of a responsible private sector replacement (investment, business analysis, and finance issues);

- Redefinition of where and how the affected employees work, and their stake in the privatization (human resource issues);
- Management of the privatization process and/or specific actions (management issues).

Preparing for privatization requires education, organization, and mobilization of four groups that must work together. Each must understand existing costs, productivity, capitalization, and other issues facing state-owned and -operated enterprises. The four groups that can make or break a privatization program are:

- Political: the executive and legislative (parliamentary) political leadership;
- Public: the consumers and recipients of public products and services;
- Government employees and managers: the group outside political leadership, typically civil service professionals, supervisors, and unskilled workers. As the performers of government functions they are the group most directly impacted by privatization;
- Business community: the local and expatriate commercial interests most willing and able to acquire, lease, or manage a government-owned and/or -operated activity.

The key to privatization is understanding and being responsive to the problems and needs of the major interest groups. Most important, these groups must understand the obligations, risks, and opportunities of privatization.

Preparing for Privatization

The process described here serves as a checklist of key questions likely to be raised at different points during deliberations. Privatization can be conducted in four phases:

- Institutional development
- Target selection
- Privatization transfer

TABLE 1   **Fourteen Steps of Privatization**

Phase I—Institutional Development
1. Organize for privatization
2. Assess political situation
3. Create private sector coalitions
4. Develop strategies and guidelines

Phase II—Selecting Targets
5. Policy review
6. Organizational survey
7. Business Evaluation
8. Strategic analysis

Phase III—Privatization Transfer
9. Estimate value
10. Issue conditions and solicitation for transfer
11. Evaluate and select successful bidder
12. Negotiate and execute transfer

Phase IV—Monitoring End Results
13. Establish regulatory and oversight mechanism
14. Monitor performance

- Monitoring of results

I have further defined the process by including fourteen logical decision points (Table 1), all of which must be addressed in the planning and implementation of a government-wide privatization program. One would find many of these steps in a well–thought out government program dedicated to the objectives of 1) cost containment and increased productivity of government, and 2) reliance upon private sector alternatives and involvement in the conduct of these programs.

These fourteen steps are not prescriptive, but are based on my privatization experience for U.S. and foreign governments. They form a

TABLE 2   **Institutional Development**

Steps	Issues
1. Organize for Privatization Initiatives	• Government vs. non-government • Define policy and program roles • Inter-governmental relations
2. Assess Political Situation	• Legal barriers • Economic constraints • Employment dislocations • Other political costs/benefits • Strengths/weaknesses of coalitions
3. Create Private Sector Coalitions	• Educating the public • Create/strengthen privatization coalitions • Develop tactics to blunt opposition
4. Develop Program Strategies and Guidelines	• Incremental vs. wholesale approach • Increase incentives (taxes, loans) • Reduce disincentives (deregulation)

checklist designed to prepare privatizers for certain questions that inevitably will arise. Each country might organize differently to reflect its own goals and development. Community resources and demand will guide the application of this checklist. If the government philosophy is to allow market forces to drive the economy and primarily to prepare with infrastructure allocations and coalition building, then it will not be necessary to wait for a crisis before privatization can proceed. A crisis does not allow much room for extensive planning. Using the steps in this checklist greatly increases the speed and degree of privatization successes.

The process is designed to encourage business, government, employee and investment groups, and other private sector interests to compete in an open and impartial manner for the production and delivery of public services. The steps I have outlined comprise a process by which a specific private sector or group(s) can replace the government enterprise economically and efficiently. What follows is a brief description of a most critical phase of the privatization process.

Institutional Development

There are four steps that lay the policy and procedural groundwork for, and begin the implementation of, a privatization program (Table 2). The first step, *organization*, begins with the definition of what the government plans to accomplish. Is the purpose the research and review of privatization feasibility, or is there a sufficient body of knowledge, expertise, and confidence within the government to develop feasible objectives, including specific privatization opportunities?

At an early stage in the formalization of program objectives, the government should designate a policy-level official to provide directives. I emphasize that this person should have access to the political leadership of government, since privatization involves regular top-level intervention and decision-making throughout the process.

Next, sufficient budget and qualified personnel must be allocated to the program. Staff size and composition will, of course, depend upon the timing and content of government objectives. Financial and staff resources must be carefully planned, justified, and utilized, as there will be constant competition for them with more established government programs. Personnel requirements include the core governmental staff and an advisory group comprised of local business people or other private sector groups, as well as other government organizations that can help shape the structure and implementation of the program.

The advisory group is an important asset, and its role should be determined early. Its jobs may include fact-finding, recommendations on policy, definition of administrative processes, establishment of criteria and identification of privatization targets, and oversight of privatization initiatives. There will no doubt be other jobs relevant to specific programs.

In the second step of Phase I, that of *assessing the political context*, it must be determined whether privatization will enable the executive and legislative leaders better to manage and oversee the production and delivery of the services. Will they be able to maintain local control, or will outside interests gain undue or monopolistic control to the detriment of local social and economic interests?

The effect on the public must also be of paramount concern. What assurances can it be given that the quality and prices of services will be reasonable? That all groups will have continued or improved access to the services or products? That there will be no precipitate termination of a service without some of the guarantees of a government operation, such as alternative sources or compensation for disrupted services?

The program's impact on government employees must be considered. What provisions can be made to protect their rights, benefits, and employment opportunities? Will they remain in government service or have preferential rights to jobs with a private firm? These questions are important to government employees and to prevent lawsuits against the government.

Finally, political assessment must include evaluations of the program's impact on the local business community. The issue turns on how much business will be available to local firms versus nonlocal or foreign entities. What sort of work (management versus labor, skilled versus unskilled) will go to each sector? Have companies made long-term investments based on a given relationship with the government? Will there be real or imagined unfair competition in the wake of government divestment to one or more firms?

In the third step of Phase I, the goal is to create *private sector coalitions* to support the privatization project. The business community must become aware of both the nature of privatization and its positive results for them individually and as a community. There should be a comprehensive public education program through which the facts about privatization are deduced and the misleading and incorrect statements rebutted. Finally, it is important to go directly to the workers, as the Thatcher administration in Great Britain does, and outline how the process would benefit them. The union members then work to educate both levels of union officers.

Once there is genuine knowledge and understanding about privatization and its effects, private sector coalitions should be strengthened.

Since it is unlikely that the entire population can be mobilized around a single issue, the best tactic is to work with special interest groups, ensuring that they do not work at cross purposes. These coalitions can generate positive pressure on local decision-makers and can be responsible for either avoidance or solution of numerous problems as the program evolves.

Related to this is the manner of dealing with groups threatened by privatization, especially government employees and others who control or benefit directly from a government-subsidized operation. They must come to understand what can be accomplished through privatization, the steps being taken to address their concerns, and the safeguards under consideration to protect the public interest.

The final step of Phase I is the development of *program strategies and guidelines*, which involves, among other things, the content and form of the administrative guidelines. There are a number of relevant issues to consider. Should the program proceed incrementally or whole-hog? In other words, should the program foresee all potential privatization actions or just selected ones? What factors and criteria should be used in the selection of privatization targets? What incentives, if any, should be considered to induce local business involvement in the program? Will there be tax changes, financial assistance, or the enforcement of social or economic regulations (antitrust laws, for example)? Overall, the balancing of incentives and disincentives will profoundly affect the degree of success attained.

Once these steps have been followed, the tasks of selecting a target and carrying out action lie ahead.

Preparing for a Specific Privatization Action

Phase II involves four steps: policy review, organizational survey, business evaluation, and strategic analysis. First it should be determined whether the government activity proposed for privatization has been the subject of a *privatization policy review*. If there has been such a review, it should be determined whether its analysis and background data can be of use in planning.

In organizing a privatization assessment, access to several kinds of expertise is critical. Technical expertise is especially important in the areas of target activity, finance, and law, especially concerning contracting and policy. Whether a permanent team is organized or individuals are retained will depend on several factors, namely the size, complexity, and availability of reliable operational and cost data, as well as operating knowledge of and experience in privatization. However the experts are organized, they will play a continuing role in all phases of the preparatory analysis.

The second step entails an *organizational survey*, including a cost analysis. What the organization does for the government and the public it serves should be clearly defined. How is it organized and staffed? What are its operating procedures, and what facilities and equipment are required to perform the activity? What are the production and performance objectives, and has the organization met them? At this point, data need to be collected, validated, and analyzed. They will serve as the backbone to a written report that encapsulates the strengths and weaknesses of the organization and ideas or recommendations for organizational improvement. The report should cover: 1) mission and objectives, 2) organization, 3) staffing, 4) definition of service beneficiaries, 5) operating procedures, 6) service size and workload expectations, 7) productivity and performance achievements, 8) equipment and facilities.

When completed, the report will serve as technical planning as well as for the ongoing education of decision-makers and the public, as it will illustrate the organization's needs, problems, and opportunities for improvement. Ultimately, this information will serve as the basis for the privatization work statement and solicitation document.

Following the organizational survey is an important aspect of the feasibility assessment: the identification and description of the targeted activity's performance costs. The reasons for doing this are to supply a knowledge bank for future discussions, to estimate service improvement costs, and to establish a cost-comparison baseline. With the help of government financial staffs, a cost assessment can be charted. It should include these eight elements: 1) labor, 2) fringe benefits, 3) materials and supplies, 4) travel, 5) equipment, 6) capital expenditures, 7) contractual services, and 8) overhead costs. If these different costs can be gathered accurately from either historic or preferably

TABLE 3   **Privatization Decisions**

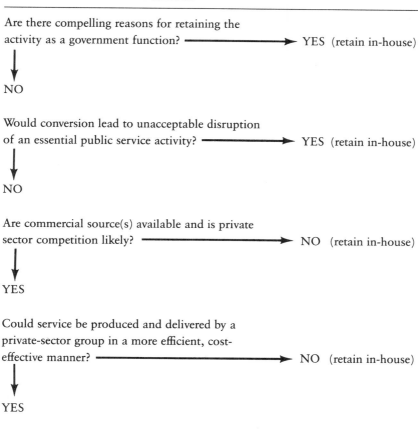

Are there compelling reasons for retaining the activity as a government function? ──────────► YES (retain in-house)

↓

NO

Would conversion lead to unacceptable disruption of an essential public service activity? ──────────► YES (retain in-house)

↓

NO

Are commercial source(s) available and is private sector competition likely? ──────────► NO (retain in-house)

↓

YES

Could service be produced and delivered by a private-sector group in a more efficient, cost-effective manner? ──────────► NO (retain in-house)

↓

YES

Prepare privatization recommendations and plan for contractual phase of privatization.

prospective operation, a good portion of the financial baselines for future assessment will have been completed.

The third step of Phase II is performing a *business evaluation* of privatization feasibility. This will be a look at business-related factors that currently and prospectively shape commercial activity. Again I have set forth a list of the issues that must be evaluated: 1) existing local capacity to perform the function, 2) capitalization burdens on both government and the private sector, 3) local business interest, 4) improved efficiency, 5) increased local jobs, 6) expanded opportunities for local business, and 7) minimal job displacement.

These first three steps of privatization assessment have been fairly straightforward and technical. The last step entails a comparative *strategic analysis* and selection of one or more options among many; these tasks are much more complex. The consequences of each option must be stated; decisions must be made about how to implement the privatization program. Can the budget support needed capital improvements in the targeted organization? Will privatization of the organization result in government employee layoff? These are a few of the many questions that will arise at this stage.

Among the principal strategic options are contracting out, sale of ownership rights (stock or title), leasing, and abandonment. Each option must be weighed in consultation with the team of advisors and support staffs. An attempt should be made to quantify the financial, legal, contractual, technical, and political implications of each strategy so they can be compared. The task is simpler than it sounds, as some of the options may not be feasible due to underlying economic, business, political, or legal obstacles, or perhaps more often, due to the nature of the target activity.

The decision tree described so far is shown in Table 3.

The final task in preparing for privatization is reporting findings and recommendations to the appropriate decision-maker. To know the degree of preparation and amount of supporting material you will need, treat this presentation as you would any other in which key decisions hinge on the facts being presented in a concise manner.

9

Steve H. Hanke

Successful Privatization Strategies

The transfer of public assets, infrastructure, and services to the private sector is a new area of public policy and finance. It is so new, in fact, that the word *privatize* appeared in Webster's *New Collegiate Dictionary* for the first time in 1983. In this essay, I will present theory and evidence that support the policy of privatization and make recommendations about the strategies required for successful privatization.

Theories of private enterprise

As I noted in a previous chapter, "The Necessity of Property Rights," theories of private enterprise provide the key to understanding the behavior of private employees and the performance of private and public enterprises. In short, private ownership creates incentives to produce goods and services in a cost-effective manner. Private managers are encouraged to maximize the value of their enterprise. In contrast, public enterprises do not generate incentives to operate in an efficient manner. Public managers and employees allocate resources that do not belong to them; hence, they do not bear the costs of their decisions, nor do they gain from efficient behavior. From a theoretical point of view, private and public managers and employees can be expected to behave in different ways: private firms will tend to be more efficient than public firms.[1]

Opponents of privatization sometimes acknowledge that while private enterprise provides goods and services more efficiently than does the public sector, various goods and services must still be supplied by the government because the poor would not be able to afford the prices that private suppliers would have to charge in order to recover their costs. This contention is incorrect. Whether the poor can afford privately supplied goods and services should not bear on the choice between private and public supply. Rather, the decision should be based on which supply alternative — private or public — can produce a given quantity and quality of goods and services at the lowest cost.

If private enterprise can supply a given quantity and quality of goods and services by using fewer resources than can public enterprise, then private enterprise should be employed. If the broad polity deems that private finance — which operates through consumer sovereignty and private charity — does not allow the poor to purchase adequate quantities and qualities of goods and services from a cost-effective private enterprise, then the polity must choose the method and level of public finance to be used to assist the poor. In other words, the choice between private and public *finance* is separable from the choice between private and public *supply*, and we can address the issues surrounding private and public supply without considering the method to be used to *finance* the desired supply.

Empirical Evidence

Economic theory as well as common sense strongly support the notion that private enterprises should be more efficient and productive than public enterprises. One question remains: Does the evidence support the theory?

Administrative functions. Studies in the United States show that administrative functions are performed at lower cost by private than by public enterprises. For example, the costs of maintaining and pursuing comparable accounts receivable are 60 percent less for private firms than for the federal government, and the federal government requires one year or more to obtain a judgment against a bad debtor, whereas private firms require only five months. As a result, the federal government writes off bad debts when they reach about $600. The comparable figure for private firms is $25.[2] The comparative costs of processing payroll checks represent another disparity. Each check issued by the U.S. Army costs $4.20. The same function is performed by large private enterprises at a cost of $1.[3] The cost of processing a claim costs Medicare, the government health insurer, about 26.5 percent more than it does a comparable private health insurer. Moreover, private claims are processed more rapidly and with fewer errors.[4]

Airlines. Evidence from Australia shows that private airlines are more efficient than public ones. Australia's public and private airlines operate with the same equipment, tariffs, routes, and departure times. However, data from 1958 through 1974 show that the private airline carried 99 percent more tons of freight and mail and 14 percent more passengers per employee than did the public airline. In addition, revenues earned per employee were 12 percent higher for the private than for the public airline.[5]

Banking. Data from a large government-owned bank, one large private bank, and five smaller private banks in Australia, show that during the period 1962–1972 the public bank had lower rates of profits to assets, profits to deposits, profits to capital, and profits to expenses than did the private banks.[6]

Custodial services and building maintenance. When custodial services for the U.S. Department of Defense were transferred to private firms, the savings ranged from 5 to 25 percent.[7] Some public schools in New York City have also transferred their custodial services to private firms, and the savings have averaged 13.5 percent.[8] From West Germany data on the cost of custodial services also show that private enterprises are more efficient than public ones. Private custodial services for government offices in Hamburg cost between 30 and 80 percent less than public custodial services. For the federal post office system, private custodial services are 30 to 40 percent less costly than public custodial services.[9]

Electricity. A comparison of ninety-five publicly owned hydro-electric plants and forty-seven privately owned plants in the United States shows that the cost per kilowatt-hour was 21 percent higher, on average, for the public than for the comparable private plants.[10]

Fire protection. There are seventeen private fire companies that operate in fourteen different states in the United States, and they operate at about 50 percent lower cost and with higher quality of service (measured by better fire insurance ratings) than do public companies in comparable cities.[11]

Forestry. Commercial forestlands owned by the United States government generate negative annual cash flows of about $11 per acre, while private timberlands, on average, generate positive cash flows. The high costs of preparing timber for sale on public lands ($80–100 per 1,000 board feet) compared with those on private lands ($10 per 1,000 board feet), in large part, explain the differences.[12] Data from West Germany show similar results as those from the United States. Public forestlands in West Germany generate negative annual cash flows (-30DM per hectare), while private timberlands generate positive cash flows (15DM per hectare).[13]

Hospitals and health care. The U.S. government, through the Veterans Administration (V.A.), operates the largest health care system in the United States. When compared with private profit and nonprofit systems, the V.A. system is much more costly. For example, the construction cost per bed is 50 percent higher for V.A. hospitals than for nonprofit hospitals. And the construction cost per bed for V.A. nursing homes is almost 290 percent higher than for comparable private nursing homes.[14] These cost differences are explained in large part by the fact that the V.A. construction programs are overadministered and wrapped in bureaucratic red tape. For example, the V.A.'s construction administration staff is about sixteen times larger on a per-bed basis than comparable private sector staffs, and the length of time from initiation to completion of construction projects is 3.5 times longer for V.A. projects than for private ones.[15]

The V.A.'s operating costs are also much higher than those of private hospitals. The average cost at V.A. hospitals is 70 percent higher per episode for acute inpatient care, 48 percent higher for surgical care, and 140 percent higher for nursing home care.[16]

Military support and maintenance. Private firms in the United States provide the same quality and quantity of services at cost savings that, depending on the service, range from 0.1 to 35 percent. In cases where all military installation support services are contracted out to private firms, the savings are about 15 percent.[17]

Nationalized industries. Nationalized industries produce a wide variety of goods and services in Western Europe. When compared with their private counterparts, sales per employee are lower for nationalized firms. Adjusted profits per employee are lower. Physical production per employee is lower. Taxes paid per employee are lower. Operating expenses plus wages per dollar of sales are higher. Sales per dollar of investment are lower. Profits per dollar of total assets are lower. Sales per employee grow at a slower rate. And with the exception of nationalized oil companies, nationalized enterprises typically generate accounting losses.[18]

Postal services. Parcels are delivered in the United States by the U.S. Postal Service and private carriers. The largest private carrier handles twice as many parcels, has lower tariffs, makes faster deliveries, and has a lower damage rate than the U.S. Postal Service. Moreover, the private firm generates accounting profits, whereas the Postal Service typically generates losses.[19]

Property Assessment. The state of Ohio requires that state and local property assessments be conducted by private appraisers, while the bulk of property assessments in most other U.S. jurisdictions is conducted by public appraisers. The average cost per assessment in Ohio is 50 percent lower than the national average. Moreover, the quality of assessments in Ohio—measured by the relationship between appraised values and actual property sales prices—is the highest in the nation.[20]

Railroads. Labor employed by America's public passenger rail line, Amtrak, is much less productive than labor employed by four comparable private lines. For example, the average member of an Amtrak work crew repairs 2,652 rail ties annually, while his private counterpart repairs 26,321 rail ties. An Amtrak crew member removes about 0.56 miles of rail annually, while a private crew member removes 4.47 miles of rail annually. A private crew member resurfaces forty-eight miles of roadbed annually, compared with only 8.84 miles of resurfacing by an Amtrak crew member.[21]

Refuse collection. A nationwide study of 1,400 communities in the United States found that, after adjusting for factors that determine costs, private refuse collectors are about 30 percent less costly than public collectors.[22] Similar results have been reported for Canada and Switzerland.[23]

Ship maintenance. Even though private commercial ships are at sea 128 more days per year than comparable U.S. naval support ships, the annual maintenance costs for naval support ships is 427 percent higher.[24]

Streets and highways. Street and highway maintenance is one of the few functions for which comparative cost analyses are available for private versus public supply in less-developed countries. A detailed evaluation of the costs of nineteen types of road maintenance functions in Brazil showed that private, contracted-out road maintenance was less costly than that performed by the Brazilian National Highway Department. On a weighted average basis, the cost for these nineteen functions was 37 percent less when they were all supplied by private contractors.[25]

Urban transportation. Considerable data on the comparative efficiency of private and public transport support the proposition that private suppliers are more efficient than public providers. In Australia, private urban bus systems cost almost 42 percent less per kilometer than do public systems.[26] In West Germany, the nationwide average cost per kilometer is 160 percent higher for public urban buses than for private buses.[27] In Abidjan, Ivory Coast, private mini-buses cover three times as many vehicle miles per employee as do public buses.[28] In New York City, the cost per vehicle hour is 10 percent lower for private than for public buses.[29] In Istanbul, the cost per seat, per kilometer, is about 50 percent lower for private mini-buses than for public buses.[30] In Calcutta the capacity cost per kilometer is 35 percent less for the private than for the public buses.[31]

Water supply. Data from a sample of twenty-four private and eighty-eight public water enterprises in the United States were used to construct a water cost model. It can be concluded from this model that average operating costs per 1,000 gallons of water produced is 25 percent lower (other cost determinants held constant) when water is produced privately than when it is produced publicly.[32]

Weather forecasting. Weather forecasting at National Airport in Washington, D.C., was originally performed by a public entity. Now a private firm performs the task; as a consequence costs have been reduced by 37 percent and the quality of forecasts has improved.[33]

Implementation

The evidence from the cost studies presented is representative of the more extensive literature that strongly supports the notion that private supply is more efficient than public supply. However, a critical question still remains: How can we best implement this desirable policy called privatization?

The question is difficult to answer, even for public officials who are sympathetic to privatization. Argentine president Raúl Alfonsín appointed Manuel Tanoira to find ways of selling some 350 of the enterprises owned by the national government. Looking to turn the construction of high-volume grain ports over to private developers, Mr. Tanoira explained, "You can't have the state running a grain port . . . . It's like flying an airplane by decree."[34] Months later, however, Mr. Tanoira reports that the Public Works Ministry is resisting efforts to allow outside bidders to remodel a vital grain port, and he charges that two of his efforts to organize privately built phone systems have been thwarted by the state telephone company's launching parallel programs of its own. "The bureaucrats are interested in one thing—holding on to their power," he says. "That a project might be better handled by someone else is of no importance to them."[35]

So even when government officials support privatization policies, the critical question still remains: How can it best be implemented? Two generic approaches can be employed: the technocratic approach and the political one. Although these are not necessarily mutually exclusive, they will be treated here as if they were. The technocratic approach requires public bureaucrats to apply techniques that are used to promote efficiency in the private sector. For example, in deciding whether to privatize the production of goods and services used and produced by the U.S. government, bureaucrats use, or are supposed to use, the Office of Management and Budget's circular A-76. This document defines policies and procedures for comparing the costs of public and private provision. In principle, if the results of an A-76 evaluation reveal that public costs are greater than private costs, then the activity in question should be privatized. By employing this technocratic procedure, goods and services used by the government should be supplied in the least-costly way. But A-76, which was first introduced in 1955, has been infrequently used. Moreover, when it has been employed, it has been highly biased toward retaining the production of goods and services by the federal government.

Another technocratic approach has recently been suggested for determining whether real assets held by public entities should be privatized. The suggested procedure requires calculating the rates of return on real assets. If these rates fall below a predetermined target rate, then the assets should be privatized.[36] Although this technique is only a proposal, there is little hope that it would be more successful than A-76.

The reason why the technocratic approach is bound to fail and why the public sector cannot mimic the private sector is that public and private property create different incentives. The owners of private property can augment their wealth only by ensuring that the least-costly production techniques are used. Private owners must also determine the rates of return on assets that they hold in their portfolios so they can decide which ones to retain or sell. Public bureaucrats do not have the benefit of these incentives when they attempt to apply private sector techniques for improving efficiency. This does not imply that public bureaucrats are neutral with respect to the application of private sector techniques and to the options of retention versus privatization, however. Public bureaucrats are biased toward retention because their job security and personal incomes are tied to retaining public assets and public production of goods and services. In short, it is in a bureaucrat's personal interest not to apply the private sector efficiency techniques in an evenhanded way.

Given these bureaucratic biases and the past failures of technocratic approaches to public sector efficiency, the most promising method for implementing privatization is the political approach. This solution amounts to nothing less than passing legislation that mandates privatization. Although it might be more difficult initially to gain support for such a political solution than for a technocratic solution, the results appear to be much more assured.

Before concluding this discussion it is important to mention that the propensity of politicians to impose price controls on goods and services once they are supplied by private enterprise can create serious problems and dramatically hinder the ability of private firms to perform. In the United States, price controls are one of the major reasons why so many activities that were originally supplied by private firms are now supplied by public entities. The process usually occurs as follows: private firms raise prices, either because service improvements are mandated or because of inflation; this brings forth demands on politicians to control prices; after price controls, the private firms find that the only way they can maintain profit margins is to reduce the quality of services; as service declines, the public becomes anxious and demands that the private firms be taken over by a public entity.[37]

Deregulation is, therefore, an important element of any privatization project. For private provision of public goods and services to be successful, demand and supply should be allowed to control prices. If it is decided for political reasons that market-determined prices are too high and that certain groups of individuals cannot afford to pay for privately supplied services, price controls should be avoided, and public finance in the form of vouchers should be considered as a way to assist individuals in the purchase of necessary goods and services whose prices are determined in deregulated, open markets.

For those who wish to advocate privatization, the rules for success should be rather clear: 1) present the theoretical arguments and empirical evidence that demonstrate the superiority of private supply; 2) keep all debate concerning the choice between public and private finance separate from that concerning the choice between public and private supply; 3) in decisions concerning private versus public supply, minimize the involvement of public bureaucrats (minimizing as well the role of private business representatives whose principal income is derived from the government); 4) make sure that deregulation accompanies privatization; and 5) enlist the substantive, unequivocal support of the highest official in the relevant political jurisdiction. This last item is the most important precondition for successful privatization, and it explains why privatization has been so successful with Prime Minister Thatcher's endorsement in the United Kingdom. Together these conditions should be expected to yield successful privatization efforts.

10

Peter Thomas

The Legal and Tax
Considerations of Privatization

Privatization is not only a political, social, economic, and technical phenomenon; it is also quite fundamentally a legal one. From start to finish, the legal and regulatory requirements effectively shape the work of privatizers and beneficiaries alike, no matter what types of action are involved. There are no practitioners of privatization law; rather, people in different fields handle privatization along with other tasks. The legal issues of privatization have not yet been addressed systematically. To make a beginning, this paper outlines the privatization modes, then reaches into the various areas of law for rules applicable to given situations.

There are as many categories of legal issues as there are approaches to privatization. The number of problems multiplies and their complexity increases as one moves from a local to an international context. This is because political complexity increases with the number and sophistication of interested parties, and since political needs are most often met by legal or quasi-legal mechanisms, the legal and tax picture grows more complex as well.

A primary operating premise is that, for all relevant parties to be protected, the requisite rules and procedures for privatization must be laid out in the form of laws and regulations. Both familiar and new rules must be adapted to a variety of specific needs. Following is a broad-brush enumeration of legal and tax concepts to consider when planning a privatization action — both good themes to follow and pitfalls to avoid.

The Range of Privatization Categories

This paper analyzes the legal and tax aspects of two categories of action: contracting out (management contracts) and divestiture (sale). Related initiatives, such as the removal of regulatory restrictions on competing activities, are covered only if such acts are part of privatization.

In contracting out, the government is acting within the context of a basic, though exotic, contract performance regime: government contracting or public service procurement. The government is paying money for the services of a private sector vendor, and the rules governing service or management are of primary concern. In sales, the principal focus is on securities law and the rules for stock transactions, since an owner (the government) is selling a transferable piece of property to new owners. Tied into this, of course, are elements of contract and property law.

Addressed first will be the universal and hence overriding legal and tax issues. Then the legal concerns that correspond to each of the two principal categories of privatization actions will be set forth.

General and Universal Legal Issues

The basic power to privatize. Before any privatization can take place, the inherent authority of the government to carry out the action must be established. Sometimes rules are based on the "commanding heights of the economy" philosophy, such as the Mexican constitutional mandate that "national strategic" enterprises must be state-owned. This law covers telephones, railways, electric power, uranium, ship building and repair, petrochemicals, steel, and airlines. In other cases, restrictions are based on momentous shifts in government policy, as in the Portuguese constitution's prohibition of divestment of previously nationalized entities.

The advantages and complications of sovereignty. One of the key factors rendering privatization legally unusual is its nature as a transaction between a sovereign entity and private individuals, human and corporate. A government possesses sovereign immunity unless it waives immunity, which protects it from many types of claims brought by private individuals or corporations. The doctrine of Act of State further shields the government. The degree to which these protections can or should be utilized is an important question, since the faith of the private sector, and thus the marketability of shares or the desirability of contracting, is at stake. Further, assumptions of sovereign debt can complicate a sale if a bond issuer subsequently adopts a new set of assumptions. The result can be fluctuating valuations and possibly litigation.

Contractual restrictions with international lenders. The conditionality of financial assistance offered by the multilateral development institutions or individual governments is always a legal consideration in privatization. Can a government use or co-mingle certain monies? Must it secure approval and oversight before embarking on a given action? On the other hand, is the diminution of the public sector a requirement or condition precedent to funding or technical assistance? Retaining outside experts is often a condition of a government's contract with the World Bank. For example, contracted-out training services are generally thought by the bank to be of great importance to government operations.

These restrictions and requirements are embodied in the loan agreements governments enter into with the providers of assistance, and they are of key importance, since in many legal systems this agreement has the force of law and overrides inconsistent text in statutes or decrees.

Dispute settlement. One of the most critical needs faced in privatization, especially in sales and contracting out, is to convince foreign participants that their legitimate grievances can be resolved fairly. This is not an easy task, as international law generally favors the government. It is difficult to make a claim against a public body because of the sovereign rights noted above as well as factors like the requirement for standing (for the party), jurisdiction (for the tribunal as well as over the parties), and a convenient locus for determination of the action.

Labor and employment concerns. The protections afforded to labor throughout the world, whether organized or not, are sufficiently strong that the legal status of current and potential employees of any affected body should always be scrutinized. The ability of unhappy employees to halt a privatization action is significant. As employees can be a valued ally in privatization, one should look closely at the particular rights granted them under domestic law, as well as the tax aspects of any transaction. Can Employee Stock Ownership Plans (ESOPs) be set up? Are vested rights preserved on transfer? Can public employees be terminated, or must they be hired by the new operator?

Monopoly concerns. One of the primary reasons for privatization is to undo the effects of a government monopoly, and care must be taken to ensure that private monopolies do not evolve. This is especially important since in most nations the law does not look favorably on monopolies or trade restraint. As one privatizes, one should investigate the powers of existing regulators (such as the Federal Trade Commission or the Justice Department in the United States, or the Monopolies and Mergers Commission in Great Britain) and determine whether new mechanisms should be put into place, as has been done with British telecommunications and gas (Oftel and Ofgase).

Financial concerns. Legal issues are often embedded in financial and economic issues—important especially where privatization is international. Currency rules, for instance, warrant concern, particularly restrictions and controls on valuation, convertibility, use and possession, and the like. Government budgetary restrictions—when does the government have access to monies, and under what circumstances—are also important. How will such constraints limit foreign participation? Are they consonant with loan agreements? Do all planned privatization agreements clearly state the restrictions?

Following are the legal and tax considerations confronted by each of the two principal modes of privatization, contracting out and divestiture.

Contracting Out

Contracting out is a phenomenon that is growing for many reasons. It is generally agreed that there are cost savings as, for example, government employment typically lacks the flexibility to respond efficiently to changes in work requirements.

The planning process. During the planning for a given privatization, it is essential that the following questions be answered: Does the government have the legal authority to enter into this sort of contract? What statutory, constitutional, or regulatory changes should be recommended? What type of contract should be selected, and what terms and conditions should be sought? Early corrections are much less costly than those attempted later.

The bid process. The most basic rule underlying the solicitation of proposals or bids from the private sector is that the statement of desires and requirements should be as widespread, transparent, and accurate as possible. When announcing a contracting opportunity, maximum participation and competition must be sought, unless there is a clear legal reason not to. International competitive bidding is the norm in conducting procurements. Legally sufficient reasons to avoid it in force-account procurements, where the World Bank is involved, relate to such things as weather-related rescheduling or transportation coordination.

After the preliminary announcement of intention, an invitation for tenders must go out. Documentation packages (including terms and agreements) should be distributed. Failure to provide each offeror with equivalent information opens the government up to potential trouble and expense. Likewise, clarification or supplemental information requested at subsequent phases of privatization must not be supplied with special consideration for any bidders. The government is bound to move forward under the terms spelled out to all bidders in the initial package, unless it reopens the bidding by providing new documents.

The evaluation and selection process. The criteria for evaluation of bids or offers must be laid out in an understandable manner. As bids are shaped on the basis of the stated criteria, there should be no deviation from this statement at any time, or the government opens itself up to legal challenge. Likewise, the collection of responses must be fair and predictable, with a set time and place, and established to allow for good-faith compliance. One must take all necessary steps to assure secrecy of the offers. Bid openings should be carried out precisely as advertised, denying consideration of late or otherwise improperly submitted offers unless these meet exceptional circumstances allowed by the advertisements.

Review and scoring of offers must be conducted by an appropriately constituted and unbiased team. As contracting out entails the hiring of services rather than the purchase of goods, bids will be evaluated more on quality, qualification, and experience than on cost. If a special review by nontechnical (policy or political) officials is desired, it must be determined that this is legally permissible; early planning could prepare government officials for whatever changes might be required.

In choosing a preliminary winner, a point is being approached at which a legally binding contract will be executed. Therefore, all issues must be carefully double-checked. Does the government have the power or funds to do all that it has promised? Did the bidder address the original request; is it able to do what it promises? Can there be full compliance with the terms and conditions? In a complex technical contracting situation, the legal requirements might prove overwhelming in a one-step process. In such cases, two-step procurement might be used, in which technical responses are sought and evaluated before business and financial presentations.

Negotiations should pin down all terms and conditions, especially the statement of work. Also, critical ancillary elements must be in place — insurance, bonds, warranties, and compliance with all laws and regulations.

The government team should include legal counsel, the person or group making policy and political decisions, and finance/budget staff. When they have all signed off, the agreement is legally ready for execution by a government contracting officer.

Monitoring and follow-up. A monitoring framework should be built into the contract to oversee all contract schedules and other terms and conditions. The government monitor acts as the eyes and ears of the legal enforcement system and takes necessary steps to obtain legal compliance or to seek appropriate legal remedies.

Disputes and termination. No matter how well structured a contract, disputes may arise or the government may wish to terminate. Clearly stated rules are necessary so that all parties will know their rights and obligations. Above all, the government must ensure fairness, sometimes called due process. In its treatment of the contractor, the government must afford a clear pathway for resolving disagreements. The first step is an informal resolution process whereby the contractor can meet with technical, contracting, and policy staff to seek simple changes.

A contracting officer would be appointed whose decisions could be appealed. The appeal would go to an administrative tribunal; then, upon further appeal, to court. The end result is either full performance by the contractor, modification of the contract to allow for changed performance and/or payment, or termination of the contract for nonperformance. While such an elaborate procedure may not be appropriate in a given national context, some procedure ensuring fair resolution of disputes is the minimum owed to contractors.

Divestiture (Sale) of State-Owned Assets

The legal issues here fall into four categories: the form of ownership, the structuring of a new organization, the arrangement with the agent or advisor working on the sale, and the offering itself.

Form of ownership. The first question at the threshold of divestment is how assets to be divested are held by the state. The state may own the assets totally, own the lion's share but not all of the assets, or own the assets jointly with private interests. The extent of ownership affects how easily the entity can be floated.

Wholly owned enterprises might be public corporations established under public law and set up as a government agency. Special
legislation may have been enacted to shape the form and powers of
the body. If so, unlike companies organized under the companies law,
they usually cannot be sold as an entity or forced into bankruptcy. A
firm under majority ownership of the government might be organized
as a limited liability stock corporation (or *société anonyme*) under the
companies law. Its autonomy would be greater than that of a wholly
owned public entity, but the powers and rights of the government would
be greater than those of the other stockholders. Joint ownership between
the government and private interests is a creature of the companies law.

Structuring the organization. While a joint stock corporation in
which the government owns shares can be privatized immediately
through the sale of shares, a public corporation wholly owned by the
government and without shares must first be reconstituted as a share
company. This is an important consideration worldwide, since most
countries do not have laws governing divestiture. There may be a need
for a new statutory enactment, or a decree may suffice.

First it must be determined how the wholly owned corporation
should be constituted — as a holding company or as a discrete entity.
It is possible to amalgamate several government organizations and privatize them into one. The next step is determining what sorts of assets
will be involved and how they will be held. All property must be
accounted for, including industrial and intellectual property such as
patents and licenses as well as real estate and machines. What sort of
legal structure will the unit have to hold its assets? Decisions must be
made on the type of share structure, the degree of capitalization, government seed capital, and guarantees of revenue, such as franchises
or licenses.

Capital restructuring of the entity in preparation for the private
sector can include such negatives as termination of the ability to draw
from a national fund for debt, and taking on debenture stock and dividend obligations. One tax consequence might be an increased tax bill
because of a lower debt charge on profiles. Further, one should investigate whether the legislation or charter underpinning the entity allows
issuance of equity, or whether monies must be raised by debt; and next,
whether debt must be undertaken with the public authorities, or

whether the private sector can be approached.

One of the most troubling legal issues facing the privatized entity is the difference between public sector accounting practices and those in use in the private sector. Examples of requirements confronted in the privatization of state-owned enterprises are: stopping the charging of supplemental depreciation; shortening the estimated useful lives of fixed assets; stopping the capitalization of assets, with a charge against revenue as it was incurred; and writing off the backlog of depreciation against reserves.

Accounting issues relate not only to individual instances of privatization but also in the larger context. Specifically, more than seventy developing countries lack a uniform accounting system, and outside participants in the process (investors, for example) are accordingly troubled. Also important is the corporation's range of liabilities. What obligations are carried with privatization of the unit? What bonds, notes, and accounts payable will come due? Will the change from public to private cause legal problems as the marketplace begins to revalue existing or proposed obligations? One must also look at the tax picture and determine whether some liabilities of the unit will be eliminated through a tax holiday, for example.

It is necessary to decide whether there will be a new corporation with a new charter, and if so, how this will be carried out. What will be the limits on operations or dealings — such as constraints on the ability of the unit to enter into contracts? Will management slots be filled before or after the sale? Will there be ownership restrictions by nationality? By the status of the potential owner of a share? By the size of the person's holdings? In some French-speaking nations, requirements and arrangements are mandated under the contract plan (or *contrat d'entreprise*) and these can be a helpful guide in privatizing a corporate entity. If the organization and the state are linked by a binding arrangement setting specific controls and relationships, such as a *convention d'établissement* or *cahier des charges*, these should be investigated, as they may lead to complications.

Finally, mechanisms may be needed to ensure compliance with relevant laws and regulations. This may even include the creation of a new regulatory body.

Use of an underwriter/advisor. The government is faced with the choice of whether to underwrite the sale or even to retain outside expertise in marketing and/or placing shares. While the decision is one of policy and market judgment, the process involves a binding agreement with an expensive professional, and has legal ramifications.

The most important advisor is the lead underwriter, who brings a team of secondary underwriters and coordinates other specialists, including law firms, accountants, personnel and operations specialists, and various technical and engineering groups. The lead role of this agent should be formalized, and all governmental liabilities for decisions should be overseen by the agent. The agreement to this transfer of authority should be in the form of a contract between agent and government. Selection of the agent should be through open advertisement and a contracting process that is fully competitive. Proposals received from merchant banks and from other candidates should be screened and evaluated by government staff on criteria including terms, schedules, and financial return, and there should be guarantees and promises to hold the government harmless in certain situations. Skill, structure, and geographical proximity of the candidates should be evaluated.

The contract award should clearly state the terms and conditions of the arrangement. The arrangement should facilitate close monitoring so that split-second decisions can be made for midcourse corrections in the interest of the government. This is critical legally since the government bears the ultimate onus of legal liability for mistakes. A rule of thumb for the apportionment of responsibility is that, if the action is a flotation requiring a large amount of research and dealing with the public, the agent stands more in the shoes of the government; if the action is a placement, the agent acts more as an adjunct and advisor to the government in dealing with the buyer, and the government's exposure is more direct. Fees will depend on the role of the firm and the size of the action.

The offering. The most common forms of divestment are:

- Outright sale of stock
    Single offer versus several portions
    Fixed price versus tender;
- Issue of convertible loan stock; and

- Issue of short-dated gilt-edged stock for later conversion to corporate entity.

These or new combinations should be investigated from the financial and marketing perspectives, then checked for legal sufficiency.

With the announcement of an action, the release of a prospectus, or the commencement of negotiations with a single buyer, execution has begun. The government and its agents should treat the prospectus as a mere announcement of an upcoming opportunity—not as an actual offer of shares—thus guaranteeing the later freedom to deny some of the potential buyers their chance to purchase should one wish to implement such a policy.

The offering documentation should clearly state the time window during which applications for share purchase can be made. This would normally be a few days at most, selected by the advisors for the best combination of timing and other factors for the government. The prospectus must set forth considerable detail on the pluses and minuses of the operation being privatized, since large numbers of people will make financial decisions based on this information. It should include data on the business environment/market; proportions of the operation being offered versus those retained by the government; any restrictions on who may purchase, and how much; and information on the status and nature of resources and assets/liabilities of the unit. The government should have a binding agreement that the property/unit is being sold without restriction (quitclaimed), and that renationalization is not foreseen. Note, however, that the government always possesses the sovereign power to take assets away from buyers under certain conditions. If an opposition power has stated that a unit will be a target for nationalization should it come to power, this statement should be included in the prospectus or in negotiations with a buyer.

It is sometimes permissible and desirable to place a portion of the offering, thus minimizing the chance of undersubscription and of large buyers holding back. However, if the purpose of privatization is to generate free-market competition, placements may be prohibited. It is also possible to offer portions of the same body of shares to different communities under different terms. For instance, a certain percentage can be offered first to the employees and pensioners, then a certain percentage of the total can be offered to institutional investors. One can make the sale of one fraction of the bloc on a "placing share" basis, in which the shares go *pro rata* to applicants, and the remainder on a "commitment share" basis, to be satisfied only if there is a balance remaining.

One can also hold back a percentage of the shares to offer them overseas. If an offer is to be made in foreign markets, the government should bear in mind that these shares would likely be covered by underwriting agreements in the country concerned. Since such agreements reflect the rules and practices of the particular country, differences in terms and conditions are critical as preparations are being made. If one is unsure about foreign markets, the potential for an underwriting contract with one's own community or central bank should be checked. Since domestic underwriters may also be uncertain that the offering will succeed in foreign markets, such agreements may include contingency clauses to protect the underwriter, such as a requirement that they are obligated to step in and purchase the shares only if the equity cannot be reallocated and sold domestically.

When applications for shares come in from the public during the prescribed period, they are collected by the agent, with assistance from the government. Although it need not be announced, the government should have a formula for culling unacceptable applicants from the pool. An example of this is the claw-back provision, with which the government can withdraw unsold shares from the oversight/control of the agent or underwriter. Often one may wish to consider a "golden share," a share to be held by the government, carrying special powers that can be employed to preserve the government's interests; for example, to keep foreign groups from seizing control of an organization involved in defense work.

When the government has decided how it wants the shareholding to look, the formula is applied and share certificates and/or refunds are mailed out. At this point the privatization has taken place, and some or all of the entity is owned by the private sector.

Special considerations. The following are a number of special considerations related to particular sales: Will the government be neutral vis-à-vis the tax consequences of the transaction, or will it grant a tax holiday? Will there be ancillary tax benefits, such as investment tax credits or incentives for small business development? Will there be special perquisites given to some buyers, such as discounted telephone service? Will some or all of the shares be offered at discount prices? Will there be balloon options, such as warrants usable in several years to buy more stock at discounts?

The government may have to give the public a binding commitment never to seek to raise its shareholdings above a stated amount— never to gain a majority, for example. Also, to ensure the value of the stock floated, it may have to pledge that it will not sell additional stock before a certain date. If there are firm legal roadblocks stopping divestiture, the concept of informal closure — keeping the legal identity but winding down corporate activities — should be investigated.

If the state-owned enterprise is a limited liability company subject to company law, it is necessary to protect against unpaid creditors who may challenge the validity of the process and maintain claims after the completion of liquidation. Determining the priority of claimants is a legal concern. Additionally, there may be a requirement for intensive discussions with lenders before any action is taken. When the government is trying to divest itself of a company with large debts, the feasibility of the government assuming the obligations should be considered. If the company has a few assets, one should see whether it is legally possible to offer a foreign lender the equity in a public corporation in exchange for forgiveness of the debt. In several recent cases, governments have capitalized an entity and framed it as a joint stock corporation; ownership was then vested in the creditor bank.

Another approach to dealing with troublesome entities is a multistep process such as has been done in India, where a number of enterprises have been turned over to state governments, which in turn are more readily able to enter into joint ventures with the private sector.

Conclusion

The legal aspects of privatization are pervasive and related to many bodies of law. While no single text can answer all questions, there are several universal points:

- In spending money or shedding public property, a government touches the roots of its law and constitution.

- One of the primary goals of privatization is protection against monopolistic behavior; this fact should influence every government action.

- Equity and fairness must be ensured for all parties, both among themselves and with regard to the government.

- Equitable compensation for property and increased efficiency of operations are the principal objectives to be realized by privatization. The law on trusts provides a reasonable foundation for evaluating a government's activities. Privatization can contribute to both the perception and the fact of government's fulfilling its fiduciary responsibilities.

11

Ted M. Ohashi

Marketing State-Owned Enterprises

The motives prompting privatization can bear significantly on its marketing. The range of motives extends from the very practical to the philosophical, including the following:

Immediate cash income. Many governments are currently experiencing budgetary deficits. The sale of state-owned enterprises (SOEs) or state-owned assets (SOAs) is an alternative to raising taxes or incurring further debt;

Immediate foreign exchange. Some governments suffer from a lack of foreign exchange, and a sale of SOEs to foreign investors can provide a possible solution;

Future cash income. Future tax revenues or creation of incremental employment justify even giving away SOEs when they are otherwise unmarketable;

Settlement of foreign debt. Where restructuring and/or refinancing foreign obligations frequently increases debt and extends it further into the future, equity from SOE or SOA sales can effectively retire the debt;

Encouragement of industrial development. A government's privatization of land, mineral rights, an idle plant, or other assets can encourage industrial development;

Encouragement of foreign investment. The same assets can be used to encourage development with foreign participation. This works particularly well in those instances where foreign technology or expertise is an essential ingredient. Where the asset is real estate, a physical plant, or extractive mineral rights, the domestic government never really loses control. Reasonable application of the legislative process ensures that, even in the absence of ownership, ultimate control rests with the host nation;

Efficiency of operations. Since innumerable studies under varied sponsorship have recognized competitive markets to be sterner taskmasters than are government bureaucracies, privatization is attractive to governments seeking to lower the cost of services. The most commonly privatized services are airlines, railroads, resource operations, and financial institutions. As pointed out above, ownership is not required for control. A regulated airline is effectively controlled; graduation to a deregulated airline may be several years in the future;

Development of capital markets. As an integral part of a long-range plan to develop domestic capital markets, privatization fuels increasingly sophisticated and broadened entrepreneurship while enabling the government to maintain some control over the rate of development;

Education of the public. Even in developed nations with sophisticated capital markets, the average person's level of financial understanding is low. Increased participation in market processes through privatization stimulates transferees to understand those processes; and

Pursuit of philosophy. Privatization may be motivated purely by the idea of free enterprise and a government's determination not to compete with the private sector in ownership or enterprise.

Marketing Devices: A Checklist

Other factors must be reviewed to decide on an appropriate marketing approach and to eliminate methods unlikely to work.

Type of transferor. A direct transferor implies asset ownership by a national government. In such cases the government is in direct control of any enabling legislation that may be required, such as relaxation of foreign ownership restrictions. Indirect transferor implies that the asset to be privatized is owned by a government agency or a state or local government, for instance. Enabling legislation must then be coordinated with senior levels of government;

Type of transferee. Privatization to a second-party transferee — employees, management group, community, and so forth — might frequently touch on social costs, such as where employees attempt to purchase a business to save their jobs, where management proposes a leveraged buy-out of an SOE, or where a community offers to buy a facility to preserve its use for local residents. Third-party investors are more often concerned with potential financial returns;

Nature of transferee. Active transferees would intend to participate in the enterprise after privatization, which would normally involve an active role for the transferor as well, in the form of subsidies or government-sponsored plans such as Employee Stock Ownership Plans (ESOPs). Passive transferees may be less likely to require an ongoing role for the transferor, although factors such as subsidized borrowing costs may be involved;

Nationality of transferee. Domestic transferees are unlikely to pose special problems, though foreign ones could. For example, restrictions against foreign ownership, exchange controls, and so on may have to be changed, as existing laws may preclude foreign investors or the free flow of currency needed to make the investment or facilitate the outflow of profits from the investment;

Type of enterprise. Existing enterprises usually have the fewest problems for privatization, but may have to be refinanced or reorganized. Newly created enterprises may create a wide range of potential problems, which can be alleviated through careful consideration of the nature of the new enterprise;

Nature of enterprise. A single-line operating company would be well suited for a second-party transferee, whereas a passive, third-party investor might prefer a multiline (diversified) holding company;

Condition of enterprise. Condition has an obvious bearing on several issues. A poor enterprise that is not marketable might be a small part of a newly created enterprise under a holding-company format. Passive investors, especially foreign ones, will normally be interested only in opportunities based on short- and long-term returns, and will therefore consider only operations or assets that are neutral or good, unless significant inducements are provided;

Type of transfer. In these times of budget deficits, the transferor may insist on immediate cash returns, and indeed may originally have been motivated by this consideration. A neutral transfer might be of the share-giveaway type, which can be done as part of a long-term capital-market development program with the government looking to a long-term repayment from future tax revenues. Cash from the transferor might be required where a joint venture forms part of a privatization, for example, with the government motivated by potential development and employment;

Extent of transfer. A complete or pure privatization may be preferable where the government is prompted by a desire to improve the operating efficiency of the unit. A partial privatization may be preferable where the government does not wish to vest complete control in private hands, or where transfer of ownership is done in the interests of satisfying a debt to a third party, especially if that third party is foreign;

Pricing of transfer. Where the asset to be privatized has an established market price, as is the case with common shares or real estate, the solution is easy, as is the share giveaway, where value is irrelevant. Pricing is a key variable that can be used to encourage participation, and in some cases undervaluation may be used to achieve certain ends;

Type of market. As a rule, in a free market virtually any of the options to be considered is possible, whereas in a controlled market the choices are more restricted, and enabling legislation may be required;

State of environment. The environment will have a major bearing on the approach to be taken. Given sophisticated markets and financial institutions, share sales or the use of other securities may be possible. The less sophisticated the environment, the more restricted the possible approaches; and

Condition of environment. Market conditions are obviously important. A good asset may be privatized under poor market conditions, whereas a poor asset may not be privatized under favorable market conditions.

This checklist can be useful in three distinct ways. First, it will reveal in relatively short order whether a privatization is possible. It will identify bottlenecks or showstoppers, and it will immediately focus attention on the critical factors that must be addressed. Second, it will quickly eliminate the variables that either do not or cannot apply. Finally, it will identify a short list of decisions that need to be made and indicate who needs to make them.

Combining Methods and Motives

The permutations of methods and motives for privatization are close to infinite. As a result, the points above can be used to stimulate discussion and to rough out potential privatizations in specific cases. Within the context of an actual case, it may be helpful—indeed necessary—to be imaginative in the approach. The less conventional issue may require a more unconventional plan. This is particularly true in less-developed countries (LDCs). The privatizations that have been undertaken in industrialized countries do not address the problems of unsophisticated or undeveloped capital markets.

Given an absence of operational indigenous markets in many LDCs, there are considerable constraints on the range of alternatives that can be employed. In considering the underwriting and sale of common shares to a domestic third-party investor, one normally assumes the existence of an active and sophisticated investment banking and brokerage community, extensive communication of financial information, credit facilities, and a reasonably knowledgeable and receptive investor community. Any or all of these may be lacking in an LDC; therefore, normal privatization techniques will not work. In such cases, innovation and imagination in planning divestitures become more important than an analysis of past approaches used by industrialized nations. If an LDC is to undertake privatization and stimulate the growth of domestic capital markets, the devices employed in the process should be creative.

Marketing Devices: The Alternatives

Although the financial infrastructure assumed to be available in industrialized countries is not always available in the Third World, the advantages of privatization are greater for LDCs, and there may be a greater sense of urgency in these cases; given the dual objectives of LDCs in privatization, virtually any financial arrangement should be considered. It will also be advantageous to examine less-often-employed features of financial agreements and to be completely flexible in their application. The following are some alternatives.

Common shares. As the basic unit of ownership in a corporate structure, the common-share issue has the advantage of simplicity. By the same token, the sale of common shares demands a higher degree of investment appeal, sophistication of financial conditions, and favorable investor psychology. Further, there is no reason to assume that all ownership is equal. There are several alternatives:

- Restricted voting. Common shares can be divided into various classes offering different voting rights;
- Conditional voting. While voting rights may be reduced under normal circumstances, full voting may be restored or effected in certain situations, such as takeover offers or successive operating losses; and
- Restricted dividends. To offset the reduction in voting rights, a priority claim on cash dividends can be provided.

Preferred shares. Generally these are recognized as a fixed dividend form of nonvoting equity. It has been suggested, for example, that in the case of privatization used to reduce foreign debt, offering preferred shares is a possibility. But variations can also be considered:

- Conversion to common shares. This can be offered after a certain time has elapsed or if certain conditions are met;

- Variable dividends. The rate of dividends can vary according to levels of domestic interest rates or profits;
- Redemption options. The shares can be redeemable at a predetermined value at the option of the issuer;
- Retraction options. The shares can be sold back to the issuer at a predetermined value at the option of the investor; and
- Voting. Preferred shares can be given conditional voting rights if, for example, dividends are not paid for a prescribed period of time.

Convertible bonds and debentures. While bonds and debentures are debt instruments, conversion features make them a form of equity. This may make them more attractive to potential investors because of their senior claim and maturity date prior to conversion. One benefit from the issuer's point of view is that a higher value can be called for the equity, as the conversion price is generally established at between 10 and 20 percent above current worth. Such securities also offer innovative potential:

- Conversion terms. They may be converted into any form of equity, with various values and schedules for exercising this option;
- Redemption options. The bonds may be redeemable by the issuer at par or some other value;
- Retraction features. The bonds may be issued with a long-term maturity that can be shortened by the investor;
- Extension option. The bonds may be issued with a short-term maturity that may be lengthened at the option of the holder;
- Variable interest. The interest payments can be made to vary with domestic interest rates; and
- Income bonds or debentures. The security may pay interest according to the profit of the venture.

Joint venture. Not all privatizations will take the corporate form. Some may be of a project nature, in which active, outside investors, domestic or foreign, participate. Examples would include the development of mining property or the construction of a manufacturing facility. Again, numerous alternatives exist:

- Standard joint venture. A project in which a government party and one other party share costs and ownership in an agreed-upon ratio;
- Earn-in joint ventures. If the earn-in concept common in the resource industry is combined with the joint venture, the result is the basic asset, and the rights to use it are provided by a government, with the investor providing the development capital and expertise. Final ownership is in accordance with an agreement;
- Performance contracts. The ratio of ownership may be decided according to some performance criteria. In mining this might be the attainment of production targets, whereas in industrial applications it may relate to meeting certain budgeted costs and time constraints; and
- Payment in kind. A situation might arise where the government does not make a cash payment for its share of costs but contributes a proportion of the initial output at a prescribed value over a fixed time period.

Asset sale. The privatization might involve an asset that is neither corporate nor project-oriented. This might be real estate, stockpiled minerals, or an unused plant, for example. It is interesting to note that the United States undertook a privatization when it began selling commodities from its strategic stockpile a few years ago. In many respects an asset sale is probably the easiest to apply in any given circumstance.

- Sale. This can take many forms. The simplest is the outright cash sale at an agreed-upon price. But the sale might be made conditional on development or improvements, and accommodated with financing, subsidies, sales contracts, and so on;
- Leasing. Again, the options are numerous, including a straight long-term lease, lease to own, or a conditional lease;
- Exchange. One asset may be exchanged for another. Where

values are equivalent, this does not really constitute a privatization, but where the government exchanges one asset for another plus financial consideration, the definition would be satisfied; and

• Grants. The asset may be given or granted another party, with the expectation that it will be compensated in the future through taxes, jobs, or a share of profits for a fixed period of time.

Second-party sales or transfers. A management or employee group offers to buy an asset or enterprise, or a community proposes an acquisition. Governments frequently become owners of enterprises because they are called on to "save" a business during difficult economic periods. If conditions improve and the business recovers, it may be a natural step to privatize. Many alternatives exist:

• Government program. A sponsored program with tax benefits, such as an ESOP or GSOP, might encourage voluntary privatization. Such programs can be easily created using existing programs as guidelines;

• Subsidized purchase. In a particular instance, a second-party group may wish to acquire a government-owned asset arranged under subsidized terms. Subsidies can take the form of tax holidays, favorable financing arrangements, or long-term contracts for output; and

• Profit sharing. A government owner may agree to fund the purchase of an enterprise by allocating a share of income to a stock purchase fund. While similar to an ESOP, the only cost to the government might be a percentage of bottom-line profit with no other subsidies or employee contribution.

There are obviously a multitude of marketing devices available when considering privatization. The challenge is to create the most appropriate vehicle given the circumstances and the motives underlying the divestiture. Knowledge of the seller's objectives and the nature of the assets to be sold will direct decisions along certain lines. For example, if capital generation is required, certain options are eliminated. If the assets suit a corporate form, then particular securities are indicated. As mentioned, common shares have the advantage of simplicity, but if the entity cannot be sold to the potential buyers at a satisfactory value, it may be necessary to use a convertible form of security to provide investors with a minimum annual interest return. The number of potential variables makes a simple, all-encompassing checklist impossible. But careful consideration of the issues will make it possible to avoid many problems and identify hurdles at the outset, which should result in a tremendous savings of time and financial resources.

12

Pedro-Pablo Kuczynski

Marketing Divested State-Owned Enterprises in Developing Countries

Three very clear lessons can be learned from privatization in advanced economies such as Spain, Britain, and several Latin American countries. The first is that privatization is a bit like marriage: you shouldn't "sort of " decide to do it. Once the decision to privatize has been made, it is important to go through with it. Second, it is very important to have clear lines of command. My company acted as a consultant in a country in which there was none. We had to report to three different ministers and several committees. This made the whole process unmanageable, and in the end, of course, it was a failure. The third crucial lesson is that there must be a major effort toward education, particularly of political opinion, not just for politicians, but also for the trade unions, parliaments, and so on.

I shall divide my thoughts on privatization into four basic areas: the steps in the process, valuation, the marketing, and the sale itself.

Steps in the Process

As far as the process is concerned, it is obvious that we must start with its feasibility. There are certain enterprises that are unfeasible to sell, reprivatize, or transfer to the private sector for the simple reason that they have no worthwhile assets. Their liabilities far exceed their assets, and it would cost the public sector more to sell them than simply to close them. So we will assume that we are talking about a feasible sale. In addition, we will assume that the sale is to either an individual or a group; public stock issues are practical only in the larger and more advanced countries.

The second question is how the enterprise should be structured so that it can be sold. There are a number of important points to bear in mind. One is the question of who will assume the debt obligations. Many enterprises to be privatized suffer from extremely unfavorable balance sheets, with debt/equity ratios of, in some cases, forty or fifty to one. Clearly they cannot be sold that way. Someone has to assume the debt, and it becomes quite a job to show the authorities that they are better off selling and assuming some of the debt than keeping it in the public sector and continuing to take losses. But this is not immediately obvious, and depends crucially on the structure of the debt assumption.

Another important factor is the tax and social security liability that in many enterprises has not been fulfilled, as well as the unfunded pension liability. Very often one finds, once the accounts are inspected, that the companies are delinquent in various contributions to the state. It is usually assumed that debts to the state should be borne by the buyer and not be forgiven, or that some form of gradual payment should be made, whereas commercial debts are negotiable. But this depends very much on the case of the particular company.

Another important point is that a company may have hidden assets. If you look at the accounts, everything is depreciated, so you do not really know its commercial value. In one case a company in Colombia had a substantial negative net worth, but its major asset, a beautiful piece of land in the center of Bogotá, was not shown on the books at its market value. The company itself, which made appliances, was worth nothing, but the land, of course, was worth a great deal. Other hidden assets include trademarks, patents, royalties that have not been exploited, and so on.

The final important point in restructuring is deciding whether the company should be broken up. The parts are sometimes worth far more than the whole. A shipping company may be worth very little, while its terminals may be worth a lot. An airline's landing rights may also be worth a great deal. One must make a very thorough analysis of a company's finances to know what is hidden, what is worth something, and what the debts are.

Once that is done and a strategy has been developed for the marketplace, projections of various alternatives must be made. Here many developing countries run into a major problem: price controls. A price-controlled market will tend to bring down the value of an enterprise because the prospective buyer is being sold a lot of difficulties in getting his prices right.

Depending on the outcome of these projections and whether the salespeople can convince the government to change policies, it may be possible to prepare a sales brochure. As its name suggests, the sales brochure is meant to sell this asset or company, and must be prepared accordingly. It must be easily readable and accessible and be illustrated. It must have good accounts. It should be easily summarized for those who are busy. Too often, sales brochures have very little information; the accounts do not go back more than a year or two; they are not prepared using standard international accounting practices; the projections do not go far enough into the future; and they give no idea of the physical facility. A good sales brochure should avoid these pitfalls and be prepared with care.

Valuation

On the subject of valuation, there is no substitute for a realistic price, which is what the market will pay. Obviously, replacement cost is one way of valuing, though it is usually not terribly relevant. It *is* relevant, however, for political opinion. People say, "If we had to build this thing over again, it would cost us so much." Of course, the answer is that if they had to build it over again, they probably would not build it, and therefore they would not have to sell it either.

Book values are another important measure, particularly in countries where the comptroller general or the general accounting office tends to consider these things. In Peru, for example, the comptroller general has immense power—or at least thinks he does—and always looks at book values. Yet book values can be irrelevant. For example, an oil company may calculate its value at $25 a barrel while the actual price is $15. The best way to value a company is to calculate its present and future earnings and those under a potential buyer. For example, a gas pipeline company engaged in merging with an oil company may not at the moment have substantial value in terms of its earning power. But if it is merged with a company that has gas fields with no outlet, its value may increase dramatically. The total earnings that this company may represent to a buyer must be calculated; that will give a fairly precise idea of what sort of buyer the sale should be oriented toward.

The earnings should be looked at in terms of the "times earnings" or "times cashflow," depending on what is important to the seller and the buyer. Clearly, with nominal interest rates at very high levels in many countries and real interest rates in the 30 percent range, anything that is valued at more than three times earnings or three times cashflow is clearly unrealistic. If you can earn 17 to 18 percent with a junk bond in the United States or 11 to 12 percent with a U.S. Treasury bond, you know that a potential buyer can invest his money in very safe instruments at six or seven times earnings. Any valuation that tends to go higher is trying to sell hope in the future, but is not really selling reality.

In the end, comparisons must be made with similar transactions. This is easily done in the United States, which has a very large market indeed; it is not so easily done in a developing country, where such sales have not taken place and where the markets are small. On the other hand, if a soft-drink company is being sold, one knows there is a certain price per case in the international market. If a mining company is being sold, there are certain ratios that are very well known. All of these comparisons will give a range. We are engaged, for example, in selling a company in Brazil that has a range from $50 million at a very high discount rate to $200 million, which represents a rather rosy view of the future and a rather low discount rate. The valuation exercise simply gives some parameters; a precise valuation is fairly difficult.

Marketing

The next step is to decide whether one should look for many potential clients or only a few. If it is a firm or economy of any substantial size, many potential clients are preferable. In the case of a Spanish sherry enterprise we sold recently, there were 148 potential clients. We ended up with five or six who were serious. But one finds that one must turn over every stone. If a buyer feels he is in a monopoly position, he will exploit it to the hilt and make a very low offer. One has to stimulate competition, and the more people one talks to, the better, so long as one follows strict investment banking principles, one of which is confidentiality. Otherwise it will appear that the sale is a desperate one, and that everyone and his brother is being sought. Any party that is reasonably interested should sign a confidentiality agreement, which is fairly standard. In this country and in Europe, it works. In a developing country it works only partially, because there are small markets and everybody knows what everybody else is doing in the end. However, it gives at least the government and seller some protection to have such an agreement.

One other aspect of marketing is whether one should conduct an auction. This method can be dangerous because it tends to freeze the price at whatever was offered in each envelope. You must have the legal flexibility to have an auction followed by negotiation. If it is only a simple auction, you will find that the price you get is much lower than if you are able to negotiate one bidder against the other. It is terribly important to be able to carry the process one step further and turn it into bargaining if the property or business is sufficiently attractive. In a number of developing countries, however, buyers do not like that. They feel they are being manipulated by an aggressive New York investment banker. They are used to buying and selling companies on the golf course, and they do not really like somebody bidding up the price.

But that is essentially the sort of function that we have, because in the end we work for our client; in the case of a reprivatization, that client is obviously the government. So in the end it is important not to have fixed auctions that end with sealed bids on a particular day, because they will not yield top value.

The potential buyers who have been identified may dwindle to only one or two. In selling the retail stores that belonged to the government of Spain, we approached forty-eight interested parties, received expressions of interest from thirty, and ended up negotiating with two. Tax credits are extremely important in these negotiations. They may be transferable — they are in most countries — and can be worth a lot of money. If the tax rate is 50 percent, this can double the price for every dollar of tax credit that you are making available.

Remittance rights on capital are also important. For example, in Brazil a number of multinational companies have large *cruzado* deposits that they cannot withdraw because they have already used up their remittance rights. Such companies are always on the lookout for others that have remittance rights. The company that you are selling may be worth very little on the books, and the valuation that you come up with may be very low indeed, but the company may have the right to remit $50 million. Given the opportunity cost of foreign exchange in a debt-ridden country, that right may be worth a lot of money.

Sale

In evaluating the offers, it is important that buyers actually put up a substantial amount of cash. If they are not putting up much cash, they should have a first-class bank guarantee behind the payments they will make. Their assumption of debt also has to have certain guarantees attached to it. Otherwise there is a risk of getting adventurers as buyers. They buy the company, and six months later they are back at the treasury saying, "This company is bankrupt. It really wasn't what I thought it was. I'm returning it to you."

The crucial part is negotiation of the offer with the buyer. Very often at that point, politicians try to influence the sale one way or the other if there are not clear lines of command. The committees one reports to are composed of people on one side or the other who are in touch with some of the buyers or politicians; the negotiation becomes complicated; there are no secrets and everything leaks out in the street. So the negotiation should be quite short. Anything that drags on for more than two or three months never gets done. We have seen sales that were prolonged due to conflicts between ministries, or the buyers were trying to use influence, and after three months it became obvious that the sale would not happen. The sale must be done fairly quickly and aggressively to nail down the buyer and be sure he is able to deliver, at the same time using the government to help him buy the company. Very often whether a purchase can be made will depend on whether the buyer can get some sort of financing.

I believe that some of the programs of the international agencies are too complicated and have too many studies and not enough practical reality. Eventually you must sell. You cannot study forever. Therefore things should be kept simple and realistic.

There are also sometimes rather convoluted forms of selling in two or three steps, which complicate the process. Things have to be kept simple and realistic. They have to be kept decisive by having somebody in the government who is willing to stick his neck out and back up the effort; otherwise privatization will never happen.

13

Financing Privatization

Privatization usually requires two phases of financing: first to support the transfer of ownership, then to ensure the continued operation of the new company. In the aftermath of transfer the company moves from the credit category of sovereign risk to that of commercial risk. Financial provision must be made for transition of the enterprise to private ownership.

Several internal and external factors affect the method of privatization, and thus its financing requirements. The overall quality and size of the business are major factors. The availability and organization of the country's capital markets and banking systems also affect financing. So does government willingness to permit foreign private capital shareholders. The availability of private domestic capital is also important, and depends on a tradition of equity investment and risk taking by local capitalists.

Once privatized, the enterprise is likely to need a combination of long- and short-term capital for modernization and the purchase of equipment and technology. There will also be a need for revolving lines of credit to finance the daily operations of the enterprise. Transitional funding will be needed to cushion the loss of such government funds as subsidy payments, capital contributions, guaranteed loans, and lines of credit that often finance state-owned enterprises (SOEs), particularly in the Third World. The SOEs might also have received international loans from agencies such as the World Bank, the Inter-American Development Bank, or the Asian Development Bank, with government guarantees that are usually unavailable once the entity has been privatized.

Let us consider in some detail how the transfer of enterprises from government to private ownership can be financed. Environmental factors that affect how such a transfer can be financed include:

- political receptivity of the country to permitting the free flow of domestic and foreign capital;
- the interrelationship of the country's capital markets to those of the rest of the world; for instance, whether the shares of companies from the privatizing country are readily listed on stock exchanges in Tokyo, New York, and Frankfurt;
- a viable and regulated securities market within the country;
- sufficient private capital within the country to purchase the shares of the enterprise; and
- the international creditworthiness of the country for access to medium- and long-term markets, so that privatization can be financed through, for instance, investment bank underwritings, Eurobond issues, underwritings backed by the World Bank, Eurodollar medium-term loans, and financing by other multinational development institutions.

For countries with advanced and viable capital markets, where the distribution and exchange of stock is done on a regular basis through a well-regulated system, privatization can be accomplished by selling the shares of the company through the stock exchange. The enterprise would have to be attractive in order to compete for investors. Sale on the stock market has been accomplished by the British government in the cases of British Telecom, British Gas, and more recently British Airways. The Conservative government's privatization program is exemplary, using as it does the free capital markets of Britain and the United States for the benefit of the British taxpayers, the investors, and the companies.

In the sale of British Gas, some of the stock issue was reserved for individual investors and the balance was sold through financial institutions. The fact that Britain and the United States have well-established and -financed securities markets has made privatization possible through existing procedures. This is also the case in France, where Prime Minister Jacques Chirac began the process of privatization soon after winning the parliamentary elections in 1986. Large French SOEs, beginning with the financial institutions, will be privatized in Paris through *la Bourse.*

Utilization of existing capital markets has the considerable advantage of financing privatization through existing mechanisms. Furthermore, it places shares of the enterprises in the hands of the public as much as possible, thus assuring a certain amount of popular support for the company. In the cases of British Airways, British Gas, and British Telecom, thousands of British citizens who previously had not been investors and never had a piece of the action in that nation's industry have become proprietors of very important British companies. For the government an economic advantage of privatizing through the stock market is that bidding can drive the price upward and provide the enterprise with additional capital.

Some government financing and support may be needed to prepare a company for sale if the enterprise is not currently profitable. This may be accomplished through such measures as selling excess assets, sizing down the enterprise, infusing government funds to improve the capital base of the company, and hiring management from the private sector to improve operating efficiency and bring about a market-driven philosophy. British Gas was an attractive investment, and the British government had little to do to prepare it for sale. But Jaguar and British Airways needed restructuring to improve profitability.

In countries where the government does not impose nationality restrictions on stockholders, selling shares of the denationalized entity is much easier, as more buyers can bid for ownership. The more willing the government is to allow the maximum amount of capital to flow into the enterprise, regardless of nationality and methodology of investment, the easier it is to launch the company successfully. In the case of British SOEs, for instance, shares were placed not only on the London stock exchange but on the European and American markets as well.

Brazil and Argentina have some ability to place shares of government enterprises in the hands of domestic investors, but they have policies restricting foreign investment in potentially attractive companies. Such policies not only render privatization more difficult, but deny the country needed capital, technology, and managerial talent.

Privatization through existing stock markets is limited in some less-developed countries (LDCs) by the absence of a tradition of popular investment in common shares, as well as by a shortage of investment capital, caused by high inflation with its resultant negative effect on the accumulation of domestic savings. Privatization of SOEs through public distribution of shares is not so easy or efficient in those countries as it is in Great Britain and France, but it should not be discounted; encouraging it promotes popular participation in stock ownership.

One method of transferring ownership without a stock market is through auction, the process of open public bidding. The enterprise is first appraised by independent accountants. The minimum bid price is announced at the appraised value, and interested investors are invited to make a sealed bid. There can be two-part bidding, where the financial and technical qualifications of interested investors are reviewed first, then finalists are invited to make a monetary bid in the standard fashion. The process is designed to ensure purchase by investors who can give the company a heightened chance of commercial success. The disadvantage of sale by auction is that the goal of democratizing the company's ownership is not accomplished, since shares are placed in the hands of only a few investors.

Another method of transferring ownership is the negotiated sale of the SOE to preselected financially able parties. Again, the process begins with outside auditors establishing the value of the business. Potential buyers are then invited to offer their qualifications. The government decides on the one best qualified to own the business. Terms of sale and purchase price are set in confidential negotiations.

Government Role

Our discussion of the sale of SOEs has thus far been based on the assumption that investors — whether in a capital-rich country or a poor one — are able to buy the company through their own financial resources, without fundraising help from the selling government. This is the cleanest and least inflationary method of effecting a change in ownership, and is particularly important in countries with an inflationary economy. The reality, however, is that many privatization sales in developing countries will require debt financing. A popular method is the leveraged buy-out. Shares and assets of the corporation are pledged to a third-party lender who provides purchase financing equal to the price of the enterprise. The net cash flow produced by the business is then used to pay the principal and interest on the loan. Leveraged buy-outs are not so frequent in other places as in the United States; however, with the assistance of international financial and development institutions, this method could be adapted to the legal and financial structures of some privatizing countries.

In nations with fiduciary laws, such as common law countries, shares could be placed in a trust fund. The administrator of the trust would manage the loan on behalf of the financing party (which could be a financial institution or the selling government) and would ensure that the buyers meet all their obligations prior to the transfer of shares to the new owners upon full repayment of the loan. The ability of a privatized enterprise to obtain traditional bank financing could be restricted where the shares and assets of the company are held in trust as security for the lender. Of course, one way to assist the company is for the government to guarantee the loan. Such support should be limited, and the company should be ready to cut all ties to its former owners so that it can become a truly private enterprise.

International lending institutions, particularly development banks, can play an important role where private sources of purchase financing are lacking and the government is not willing or able to finance the sale. Where native buyers have a portion of the needed capital but not the full amount, an institution like the International Finance Corporation (IFC), a subsidiary of the World Bank, can engage in joint ventures with local investors. The IFC can participate by providing capital in exchange for an equity position in the enterprise. The IFC can also provide debt financing under better terms than commercial lending institutions can, requiring perhaps a preferred position in the repayment of its loans. Development institutions like the IFC and the Inter-American Development Bank are able to provide not only capital and debt financing, but also technical and management expertise.

Normally, financial markets in developing countries are limited to debt, rather than equity, instruments; mortgage bonds and government debt instruments are popular investments. In cases where privatization needs to be financed, the issuance of bonds secured by the assets of the enterprise is an attractive alternative. These bonds, issued by the newly privatized company, may need to carry privileged conditions to compete successfully in such limited capital markets. Some possible conditions might be government guaranty, tax exemption for interest paid on the bonds, or permission for such obligations to be official bank reserves. This method of financing has the advantages of making it possible for the government to receive full payment on the sale up front, and of providing investment opportunities to the public. It is important that the quality of the enterprise issuing the bonds give the public confidence in the investment as well as in the policy of privatization.

Although international bank loans are one way to finance privatization, for the present and foreseeable future this method presents problems because of the already heavy obligations (some in default) carried by many Third World countries and enterprises. It is not realistic to believe that private international banking institutions will increase their already troubled loan portfolios in order to provide unsecured credit to support privatization. The transfer of heavily indebted government-owned companies to their lenders has been proposed as a solution to the international debt crisis, and this could perhaps be a method of both accelerating privatization and resolving the debt crisis.

Continued Financing

Once an enterprise is privatized, continued financing is extremely important. In the already mentioned cases of British Gas and British Telecom, there was little concern about working capital, as these companies already enjoyed ample lines of credit. They also had the advantage of operating in financial markets with ample monetary and banking resources. The opposite is true in the Third World, where government businesses are marginal at best, and financial markets lack liquidity. LDC governments would have to provide for either backup financing or guarantees of private bank commitments, particularly commitments from abroad.

Working capital requirements of a business can be satisfied through the financial markets or through company profits. The most important and attractive, least expensive, and least inflationary method of financing ongoing operations is through the generation of profits. This is the most assured way of financing working capital. Profits provide internal financing and make it possible for financial institutions to risk depositors' funds. Profits make growth possible, since they can be reinvested in the purchase of capital equipment and technology. The lack of SOE profitability has been a drain on taxpayers, and has deflected resources away from programs more suitable for the public sector, areas where Third World governments prone to centralized control have shown themselves to be neglectful.

Accountability of management to the owners makes private enterprise a much more efficient and better provider to society than government-owned institutions, whose managers are only accountable to politicians, bureaucrats, and their own agendas. The need to satisfy consumer demands and the profit expectations of owners enables privatized companies to finance themselves through profits and encourage private financial institutions as well as the public to provide support.

Conclusion

Financing privatization requires planning, and must take into consideration the many factors set forth here. The process must begin with pre-sale preparations and be carried through to where the enterprise is self-financing. Many factors within the company as well as in the environment where it operates affect how the process will be managed. One thing is known: economic entities driven by goals of excellence and service to the public are more likely to succeed. It has been proven that private companies pursue these goals more effectively and contribute to, rather than drain from, the economies of their countries.

Part IV

Privatization for Development

14

Gabriel Roth

Privatization of Public Services

This paper presents examples of full and partial privatization of public services in developing countries and draws some conclusions that may guide concerned governments and aid agencies. The services considered are education, health, electricity generation, telecommunications, water supply, and transportation. The examples are taken from a book I wrote for the World Bank.[1]

Education

The tradition of private education exists in all known civilizations. When Confucius said that he would teach anybody who bought him a meal, he meant that he did not mind how much he was paid, as long as the principle of payment was accepted. The idea that education should be "free" and supplied by the state is of fairly recent origin. It became established in Europe and North America in the nineteenth century and was subsequently embraced with enthusiasm in the twentieth century by governments in Africa, Asia, and Latin America, with results that did not always meet expectations. Private education still survives in those countries because the public sector is short of funds and the private sector can offer a better product, particularly for specialized purposes and in the education of minorities.

The financing of education raises serious problems, but provision of "free" services by government employees is not necessarily the best way to deal with them. Education can be provided by private enterprise even if the financing is in the form of government grants or loans. Loan funds are particularly well developed in Latin America, where about twenty institutions cooperate internationally through the Pan-American Association of Educational Credit Associations (APICE).

If grants are felt to be more appropriate than loans, it is possible to use education vouchers, which give the user the right to purchase education up to a specified value from approved institutions. This device was used very successfully for demobilized soldiers in the United States after World War II. A similar scheme is now used in Chile: local authorities pay approved schools a specified amount for each day that a child attends, and the schools compete for enrollments. The value of this payment is on the order of US$100 a year, which may be a fifth or sixth of the fees charged by equivalent private schools. Nevertheless, the amount is sufficient to enable groups of teachers — and parents — to establish some new public schools. The Chilean voucher cannot be used to supplement fees in private schools. The system was introduced in the 1940s as part of a reorganization that devolved responsibility for the schools from central government to the counties. It was revised in the 1970s.

Health

The health sector, like education, has a long history of private provision. According to the World Bank, across the spectrum of developing countries most expenditures for health care are private. Even in cases where facilities are publicly owned and the services are free, people go to private clinics because public hospitals are undercapitalized, with no staff, equipment, or supplies. Traditional medicine is widespread in Asia, Africa, and Latin America, and the practitioners almost invariably operate on a fee basis. This is a strong signal that health care should be moved out of the public sector. Major problems include the organization of health insurance and integration of the traditional and modern sectors.

Health insurance, like education loan plans, is highly developed in Latin America. In some cases, insurance covers groups of employees; in others, insurance companies cover individuals. Health insurance can also be found in less-developed societies: in many Indian villages it is traditional for farmers to bring the local practitioner a gift at harvest time, which serves as an insurance premium for care the following year. Similar customs are found in Indonesia. The integration of traditional with modern medicine is found in many countries. In India it is supported in government medical school; in Ghana there are government programs to give modern training to traditional birth attendants, who are then allowed to charge higher fees as a reflection of their new skills. Traditional medicine is more advanced in India and China than in Africa, possibly because treatments and remedies are recorded and published, and thus made available to other practitioners for testing and comment. In Africa, on the other hand, traditional remedies are handed down from one practitioner to another under conditions of secrecy, so lessons disseminate much more slowly.

As in the case of education, there need be no conflict between government financing of health services and private production. Under the National Health Service of the United Kingdom, individuals are encouraged to choose their doctors, who are then paid an agreed amount out of public funds for each person on their lists.

Electricity Generation

One major obstacle to the improvement of electricity supply in developing countries may be the belief that the industry should be treated as a natural monopoly, and that electric power must therefore be supplied by the public sector, or at least regulated by it. It can reasonably be argued that electricity transmission and distribution exhibit such economies of scale that they can be regarded as natural monopolies, but the generation of electricity can be carried out, as in North Yemen, at widely scattered points, either for use by the generating firm or for sale. There is also the possibility of cogeneration (an industrial process that produces heat and electricity simultaneously), with electric power being sold for use by the government.

In theory, one can envisage a publicly owned and operated grid buying electricity from competing suppliers at prices that reflect supply and demand. This does not appear to be happening anywhere in the Third World, but legislation passed in the United States in 1978 requires electric utilities to buy power from certain producers if it is offered at favorable rates. The law encouraged the emergence of hundreds of small companies that generate electricity from wind or water power. In this manner, electricity could be provided in the developing world.

One method of ownership that seems to have more attractiveness in less-developed countries (LDCs) than private enterprise is cooperatives — private enterprises that are owned by the users instead of by shareholders or investors. Some will argue that cooperatives are not all that private; it is true that in the early stages they do need public support. This is because in the early stages electricity rates are controlled and usually set at below-return rates. But eventually that changes: older systems such as those in Costa Rica, Argentina, and Chile are private.

One possible source of electricity available to scores of developing countries comes from the burning of bagasse, the remains of sugar cane after the syrup is squeezed from it. In its dried form, bagasse is frequently used to provide the necessary fuel for the manufacture of sugar. With suitable upgrading of equipment it is possible to generate more power from it than is required to make sugar, and this power can be made available to the public grid. In Mauritius, for example, it was calculated that 8 or 9 percent of the total electricity needs of the island could be met by burning bagasse instead of importing fuel.

Telecommunications

In most Third World countries, demand for telecommunication services far exceeds supply, as evidenced by the high prices at which telephone lines change hands in cities where such transactions are allowed

($1,500 in Lima and Rangoon; double that in Bangkok). A recent World Bank publication posed the question, "Who or what group has decided that telecommunications investment should be constrained relative to demand by closely regulating and controlling inputs to the sector, its organizational structure, and the internal procedures of telecommunications operating entities, and by imposing numerous restrictions under which operating entities must operate?" It concluded that, rather than the users, it must be the owners, suppliers, and regulators of the services—which in most developing countries are governments.[2]

In the past, the governments of LDCs have generally decided that food, transport, power, health, and other most pressing needs should receive the most emphasis. So long as telephones were viewed as an inessential and largely luxury consumption, investment in the telecommunications sector received low priority. In the last few years, this perception of the role of telecommunications has been changing, largely because of the explosion of telecommunications activity occasioned by the technological revolution. Modern telecommunications are becoming essential to business activity—initially to compete in the international marketplace and increasingly for domestic business activity as well. This revolution is generating pressure for change in the traditional organization of telecommunications activity and in the priority it receives in the investment world. Where developing countries have such a demand for telephones that individuals wait a year for installation, there is a strong case for allowing a competitive service to operate. A good deal of discussion about reform is going on, with many different mechanisms being examined, to make telecommunications entities more flexible, commercial, and efficient.

Proposals for full-scale privatization are extremely rare, even among the most active reformers, because most governments feel that, even if it is ultimately deemed to be desirable, full privatization is too large a step to be taken all at once. Some governments are instead seeking gradual reform, through which the consequences of each change can be evaluated before the next step is taken. These reforms include 1) internal reorganization of telecommunications entities, such as changes in procurement, pricing, and management systems; 2) creation of autonomous or semiautonomous government entities to replace government ministries; 3) joint ventures and management contracts; and 4) per-

mission granted to major competitors and users to create alternative
systems and connect them to the public network.

One example of partial privatization involves a private facility
accessing the international telecommunications network and providing service to a limited number of special customers. The "Teleport"
is planned for start-up in late 1987 in the Montego Bay Export Free
Zone in Jamaica, with management and financing provided by a U.S.-
Japanese joint venture. The purpose of a teleport (of which there were
at least sixty-five existing or under development in North America in
1987) is to provide high-speed, high-quality voice and data lines for
companies engaged in telecommunications. The Jamaica Teleport is
designed to serve information-intensive enterprises in the Montego Bay
Export Free Zone, such as telephone marketing operations, reserva-
tion centers, and data entry firms. Information will flow between the
United States and the Jamaica Teleport on voice and data lines via a
Contel ASC satellite and a specially constructed ground station in
Jamaica. The price of private leased voice and data circuits will be comparable to those of U.S. domestic telecommunications operations, which
are competitively determined and therefore substantially lower than
those normally charged for international services. These low rates are
expected to make the free zone's facilities especially attractive to U.S.
firms. And many of the users accessing the operators at the teleport
will not realize that their phone calls, placed through the 800 network,
will be earning valuable foreign exchange for Jamaica.[3]

Experience with private sector operation of telecommunications
in LDCs has been mixed. In a number of countries, such as Botswana,
government-owned companies have been managed by foreign private
firms with reasonable success. Private telecommunications companies
owned by foreign interests were once common in Latin America, but
most were nationalized in the 1960s. The Dominican Republic still has
a public service supplied by GTE, but even this relationship appears
to be having difficulty after many years of relative harmony. The Philippines have a fully private telephone system that has long been unsatis-
factory, for reasons that warrant further study.

The communications revolution requires LDCs to rethink their
telecommunications strategies and make appropriate adjustments to
meet escalating needs and pressures. Increased commercial orienta-

tion for existing PTTs and an increased role for the private sector are important and highly desirable components of this adjustment. But care must be urged, as the problems are extremely complex and technology is evolving rapidly. Public interest concerns in telecommunications will always be important, so there will always be a role for the government.

Water Supply

Because of a genuine or alleged reluctance to pay for piped water in developing countries, private investors are reluctant to supply the necessary infrastructure. One way of dealing with the problem is to adopt the French system of *affermage*, whereby the infrastructure is financed out of public funds but operated by a private firm. Such systems are to be found in North and West Africa as well as in France, where there are sufficient qualified firms to ensure that cities can always solicit bids. There are different ways of bidding: the company might win a contract by being the one to quote the lowest rate of charge to provide customers with a package of services, or it might be the one to offer the lowest sum for the right to supply these services at prices determined by the government.

Among rural areas, the development of private tube wells has been particularly successful in the Indus Valley in Pakistan. In the 1940s the government installed more than 14,000 tube wells, mainly for drainage, although it was believed that improved irrigation would be a useful by-product. The Indus basin farmers preferred to have their own wells, however, and the 14,000 public tube wells were matched by 186,000 small-capacity tube wells that were installed by the private sector, 90 percent of them with no subsidy. Assessments by World Bank staff concluded that the private tube wells had been managed efficiently, imposed a relatively insignificant burden on public resources, produced returns that were economically justified, and did not lead to excessive exploitation of the aquifer.[4] Furthermore, private initiatives produced a remarkable range of ingenious inventions using cheap local materials. A bamboo tube well was developed in Bangladesh that is so cheap that several can be inserted in the same plot. Used in conjunction with an engine and pump mounted on a bullock cart, the wells can irrigate an entire farm area economically. It is not even necessary for every farmer to own a pump, because contractors emerged to serve pumpless tube wells.

Agricultural production is often constrained due to lack of water, while surpluses exist in neighboring areas. Can large quantities of irrigation water be moved from areas of plenty to areas of shortage? One of the main constraints to activity of this kind is the absence of clear property rights for water. If such rights were clarified, it is conceivable that the movement of water over long distances could do as much to stimulate agriculture in India as it already does in California. A transfer of water on the basis of property rights implies payment to the sellers at freely negotiated prices.

A move toward the privatization of domestic water supply by granting property rights has taken place in Kenya.[5] In some regions, villagers had not been paying the small monthly tax that was to be used to help operate and maintain local water supply systems. Furthermore, frequent acts of vandalism on faucets, drainage facilities, protective fences, and so on made it financially prohibitive and almost physically impossible to maintain many of the public standposts. To overcome this, public water facilities in a few areas were converted to water vendor operations, a licensed vendor paying a subsidized rate for the metered water and selling it to users by the container at a slightly higher fee. As a result of the switch to kiosks, vandalism has been greatly reduced, thus saving government funds spent for repair and replacement; a small amount of revenue has been generated; and the rate at which people apply for house connections has increased. Some people presumably felt that if they were going to have to pay for water, it might as well be convenient.

Transportation

None of the above examples is of actual public sector divestitures; the transfer of a public service to the private sector is comparatively rare, but there are some cases in transportation. In Mexico, for example, the port of Tampico was given to the workers when the government got tired of paying its deficits. Under worker management, efficiency increased markedly. However, in 1985 Tampico joined Altamira to become once again a public sector complex. Road maintenance is now contracted out to private firms in countries as dissimilar as Brazil, Nigeria, and Yugoslavia.[6]

An interesting example of urban bus divestiture occurred in Buenos Aires, where in 1951 a national enterprise known as Transportes de Buenos Aires took over all bus and rail transport operations. The services deteriorated rapidly both financially and in quality. By 1959 the service was losing the equivalent of US$40 million per year. In 1962 the situation became intolerable, and Transportes de Buenos Aires was dissolved. All the lines except the underground railway were turned over to the private companies that had been operating before 1951. Many of these companies were *empresas* (route associations) of owner-drivers empowered to serve just one route. The *empresas* governed routes, fares, and schedules, subject to rules determined by the regulating authorities. The vehicles used were typically twenty-three-seat buses, which provided a high frequency of service. Competition was created by the establishment of new *empresas* that duplicated the routes of existing ones. The microbuses still operate profitably and provide a highly praised level of service.

A different approach is seen in Calcutta, where in 1960 all bus services were vested in the Calcutta State Transport Corporation (CSTC). The CSTC suffered from managerial and financial problems and was paralyzed by strikes in 1966. In response to its need for ready cash and to public demand before the 1966 elections, the government of West Bengal sold permits that enabled 300 private buses to be operated. The buses earned a profit, although they charged the same fare as the money-losing CSTC and had inferior routes. By the late 1970s some 1,500 full-size private buses were operating in Calcutta, in addition to about 500 private minibuses. In 1985 the private buses accounted for about two-thirds of all bus trips without subsidy. Meanwhile, the CSTC, which operated similar routes at the same fares, had to be subsidized at the equivalent of US$1 million a month by a government desperately short of funds. A similar coexistence of profitable privately owned buses and loss-accruing government-owned ones can be found in Sri Lanka and in the state of New Jersey.[7]

Privatization

The impediments to privatization are many and various in developing nations. In African nations that were under colonial rule, the national capital is not strong enough to develop these institutions. The people with money and power left the country, and those who inherited public institutions are very poor and cannot afford them. The private sector is reluctant to put the little money it has into public services. Other countries worry that privatized services will not have the clout to collect from their customers. For example, garbage collection in an area with underdeveloped civic responsibility may not get paying customers; people may just dump their trash at the roadside. There are problems where existing monopolies object to competition; this can be exacerbated by unemployment, by unions, and by a lack of political will. Finally, there often exists a shortage of management.

Thus it is important for developing countries to ease into privatization, rather than perceiving themselves as in an all-or-nothing quandary. Privatization needs to be broken down into distinct pieces to be understood. Three categories seem essential: first, who determines market demand? Government can, or government and citizens can jointly, as through the use of vouchers; finally, the private sector can determine demand exclusively, as is the case with jitney services in the Philippines and Buenos Aires. Determination of demand is a form of empowerment: the very essence of the concept of privatization is greater citizen control over the level and range of services and goods production.

Second, who finances the service? The government can, or the financing can be a private-public partnership, as in user charges. And, of course, the private sector can finance privatization exclusively. Third, who provides the service? The government can, whether in a competitive framework or a monopoly. Examples of the former are contract cities in California, in which the county sheriff seeks bids against local police departments to provide local services. Production can be a private-public venture, as in contracting for private provision for a public service. Or it can be absolutely private. These kinds of distinctions are essential to find ways to ease into privatization.

Conclusion

Of the services examined, telecommunications and electricity generation probably offer the greatest potential for private involvement because of intense demand, the comparative ease of collecting payment, and the poor existing levels of service in most countries. Transportation is also a fertile field for privatization, one that is already being tilled. Education, health, and water are more difficult, because payment by government may be required. But even when services are paid for by the public sector, management of them can still be contracted out to private enterprise.

There are many examples of public services being provided by the private sector in developing countries, but very few cases of full government divestiture have been documented. The reasons for this are not clear, but it may be hazarded that, as in the United States, the pressures to retain activities that are in the "public interest" without subjecting them to the bothersome disciplines of markets are well-nigh irresistible. In the cases where ownership has been transferred to the private sector, the divestiture involved the return to private ownership of an originally private concern that had not been run successfully by the public sector. The Jamaica Teleport, with its low international transmission rates, illustrates a spillover of the consequences of U.S. deregulation into the international arena.

It may be that the most painless way of bringing about the private provision of public services in developing countries is to *deregulate* rather than to *divest*—to allow the private operation of competitive services while leaving to the public sector the operations under its control, in the hope that competition would either improve them or make it easier for them to be wound up. One may also conclude that a shortage of cash encourages divestiture—not to mention economy in the use of scarce resources—and that governments seeking economic growth should strive to abolish subsidies to failing public services. Subsidies can be designed, as in the case of the schools in Chile, to go to consumers without depriving them of their choice of supplier.

15

Ian Marceau

Privatization of Agriculture and Agribusiness

In many developing nations the parastatals number in the hundreds and thousands. In those countries in which agriculture and agribusiness are significant contributors to the gross national product (GNP), parastatals tend to be concentrated in those sectors. There are no reliable data on the amounts of investment in agriculture or agribusiness by public and private enterprises, and the data on parastatal involvement by sectors are poor. The scope of parastatal involvement in developing countries is illustrated by the following:

- In a 1983 World Bank report on state-owned enterprises (SOEs), Mary Shirley reported that in the early 1980s the nonfinancial SOE share of total domestic credit in developing countries ranged from 7.2 percent in Jamaica to 91.5 percent in Indonesia. These statal and parastatal organizations were responsible for more than 25 percent of domestic credit in most of West Africa, Burma, Bangladesh, Bolivia, and Indonesia. Fifty percent of 1980 government tax revenues in Brazil were transferred to SOEs, while the foreign debts incurred by SOEs in Peru between 1976 and 1980 totaled 31 percent of the nation's total foreign debt in 1980. Most nations show that in excess of 50 percent of domestic credit is soaked up by statal and parastatal organizations. That is a staggering percentage when one considers the low level of capital resources available for development in these countries.

- Only four sub-Saharan African countries had private fertilizer suppliers in 1981. In nine countries there was mixed private-public supply. In the remaining twenty-six countries, fertilizer was procured and distributed by the public sector. The same pattern applied to seed supply, chemical supply, and farm equipment supply.

- While most nations of the sub-Saharan region experienced decreases in per capita agricultural production during the period 1969–79, increases were achieved in Kenya, Swaziland, and Mauritius, three countries in which the private sector dominates the procurement and distribution of agricultural inputs.

Since agricultural inputs are imported in almost all countries of the region, state enterprises play a pervasive role throughout the factor markets of most of these nations, from the national arena down to the individual farmer. Combined with the marketing parastatals, the involvement of government is pervasive throughout the agricultural and agribusiness sectors.

Issues in Privatizing the Agricultural and Agribusiness Sectors

In addition to the involvement of marketing boards in these sectors, governments intervene using statal and parastatal enterprises in all facets of the agricultural industries of developing countries. State enterprises are involved in the procurement and distribution of physical inputs—

seeds, fertilizer, chemicals, and equipment. Proponents of the system claim that in less-developed countries (LDCs), with their limited resources and scarce foreign exchange, centralized coordination is necessary for effective delivery of inputs to those producers most important to the economy. But the fact that the sub-Saharan nations in which the private sector is ascendent have increased their per capita agricultural output while those with extensive governmental involvement have experienced decreased per capita output strongly suggests that the proponents of centralism are incorrect. The experience of private fertilizer distributors in Bangladesh in recent years provides further evidence that the private sector can handle production inputs successfully in LDCs.

Privatizing procurement and distribution of production inputs involves development of:

- methods of devolving the monopoly powers of the parastatals to private traders;
- mechanisms for giving traders access to the capital needed to finance procurement and marketing of inputs. Of particular importance is access to foreign exchange at real exchange rates;
- the role of government in providing the transportation and communications infrastructure necessary to facilitate traders' access to rural and other markets; and
- the proper role of government in facilitating availability of credit, enabling farmers to buy production inputs at nonsubsidized market prices.

Options available for privatizing production inputs include:

- devolution to the private sector of parastatal activities. This would result in elimination of the state's monopoly powers. This can be accomplished only by a government policy decision. The case of Mali and the removal of the monopoly powers of the grain parastatal OPAM provides a model. The key to success in inducing the government of Mali to hand the business over to a free market was the provision of guaranteed financial assistance to buffer the privatization process. A similar approach could be used for other parastatals;

- facilitation of private sector access to the capital required to fund procurement and distribution of agricultural inputs by removing restrictions on the ownership of or access to the foreign currencies needed to purchase these inputs abroad; of importance here is the requirement that the artificial exchange rates maintained by many countries be abolished;

- use of conditional aid to change the urban emphasis of most government policies to ones that share resources more equally with rural regions. My 1985 survey of sub-Saharan Africa has shown that the likelihood of privatizing infrastructure services in developing countries, especially transportation and communications, is extremely remote. This is the most feasible option to facilitate privatization of other components of the agribusiness sector; and

- establishment of rural credit programs that charge market interest rates and are backed by government loan guarantees. This is the most attractive option to provide farmers with access to enough credit to purchase production inputs at market prices. Donors could consider concessional assistance in the early stages.

Land and Capital Investments

Given the availability of the necessary inputs and financing through the private sector, the key to privatization of the agricultural and agribusiness sectors is the sanctity of property rights. Without the guarantee of long-term interest in the land required for farming, and the capital goods needed to engage in business, privatization will fail. Where a communal base of agricultural production persists, attenuated ownership persists, and significant improvements in agricultural policies (including the elimination of marketing boards) cannot be expected to have the same benefits that they might have where ownership is securely vested in individuals.

Conversely, in those few African countries where governments have invested in land titling and expanded individual ownership, marketing boards and pricing policies tend to be less oppressive than in countries where communal production has not been systematically addressed. Reforms are necessary to guarantee property rights and individual use of property in the private sector. Governments must guarantee either the right of ownership and reasonably unfettered use or the right of access to resources over the long term for reasonable purposes.

Reforms in this area could include:

- constitutional or at least statutory protection against expropriation of private property, implemented and protected by appropriate judicial procedures; and

- statutory rights of resource use under leasehold or other legally enforceable forms where private ownership is not appropriate, as in tribal communities. This practice is common in the United States, where forest lands are often publicly owned while guaranteed private use has allowed a long-term forest products industry to develop.

Privatization of Marketing Boards

In most countries the cost of running marketing board bureaucracies is a major contributor to the shortage of LDC financial resources that could be used to pay a truly reasonable return to farmers. Often these organizations have as their primary purpose the "employment" of the politically and otherwise favored members of society and the provision of income to the powerful. Their role in the agricultural productivity of the nation is at best secondary. Thus, the following price-related issues need to be considered in privatizating marketing boards.

Production management. In addition to their roles in setting and administering prices, marketing boards are often used to enforce production quotas—usually production ceilings, but sometimes minimums imposed by cropping area regulations. The limitation of production is a common feature of the agricultural policies of developed nations. These ceilings inevitably create economic inefficiency, which is exacerbated by subsidies paid to compensate farmers for reduced output. In cases where minimum cropping requirements are imposed, inefficiencies are introduced by forced product substitution and associated inputs, and by the resulting price signals. Therefore, the production-related issue in privatizing the boards is the role and appropriateness of quotas in the agricultural economy.

Marketing of products. Marketing boards are usually the sole legal purchasers and sellers of products within their purview in developing countries. Fortunately for private sector interests, the enforcement of the boards' monopoly role is usually ineffective, the result being a flourishing informal market in which products reach consumers through parallel, illegal marketing channels. However, when the free market is rendered illegal it is forced to stay small and thus ineffective relative to its potential. Governmental efforts to use official marketing channels to eliminate or restrict the role of private operators, while largely unsuccessful, usually result in the misallocation of national resources and the introduction of costly inefficiencies.

All governments intervene in agricultural markets to some extent, and this is justified where governmental involvement is necessary for reasons of social equity and market stability. The issue to be addressed in privatizing marketing boards is the degree to which public agencies should be involved. Price stabilization and buffer programs are a valid public responsibility, whereas involvement in direct trading should be left to private interests. The question is how to accomplish this end. Options include the following:

- recurrent financial assistance from donor agencies to back up government efforts to stimulate the private sector. Especially important would be the provision of funds to support higher producer prices and to compensate consumers for the reduction of subsidies;

- an initial financial contribution from foreign sources, based on a host government schedule, to bring producer prices and consumer costs into equilibrium by phasing out governmental interventions; and

- the institution of consumer vouchers (food stamps) where a government can derive the same value from them as from price-setting, at substantially less cost to itself and the economy. If the government wants low consumer prices and insists on setting them, consumer vouchers would allow producer prices to float. The value of issued vouchers would vary, in turn, as corollaries of the difference between market and mandated prices (except where the latter exceed the former). This consumer subsidy could be phased out, without production disincentives, in accordance with a fixed schedule and/or increases in production.

The likelihood of financial assistance by donor agencies is low, since it involves the unattractive prospect of long-term commitments without any real leverage to induce the government to change its policies. The second alternative, finite and conditional financial assistance, is more likely to find acceptance. In fact, this is precisely the model followed by the donors group assisting Mali in privatizing OPAM, and appears feasible for adaptation to different marketing boards in numerous countries.

Conclusion

The options outlined here concern the macroeconomic factors that emerge from a particular theoretical background. Many LDCs continue operating under the old industrialization theory of development, favoring the industrial sector over the agricultural. This means squeezing the latter for "excess" labor or savings to invest in industry—considered more productive and the engine of development—by holding down agricultural prices and establishing import tariffs favorable to industry and unfavorable to agriculture. Import substitution policies, still prevalent in many LDCs, are part of this theory of development and have impacts on both agricultural input and output markets. One impact is the overvaluation of domestic currency that usually accompanies import substitution, making agricultural exports less competitive. Along with making purchase of imported agricultural inputs more difficult and domestic inputs more expensive, control of foreign exchange allows these countries to allocate scarce foreign exchange to the favored industrial sectors.

Supply-side policies, which are used to increase incentives for individual production, should be expected to reap quite different consequences in different institutional settings: positive where individual property and contract rights are established; not positive where those rights are attenuated. The elimination of government intervention in agriculture may be a necessary condition for increasing productivity and production, but it is sufficient for rendering those effects at an above-subsistence level in lieu of government intervention in the land market to achieve reform. Even with communally based production, Africa suffered droughts without famines until it experienced the interventions in agriculture of newly independent governments. Eradication of those interventions is essential to the avoidance of widespread starvation. But if more is desired — agricultural production above subsistence and complementary to economic growth in a developing society — then the institutional basis of production must be addressed. In short, policies which would increase incentives for production make sense in individual terms, and are unlikely to realize their intended effects where individual ownership is not established. Incentives for individuals must promise individual benefits, which require individual ownership.

Positive changes in commonly cited bad government policies are more likely to occur where they are accompanied by government successes in establishing and expanding private ownership rights. Where this is achieved, individuals with an interest in making those other changes emerge, and a political constituency is formed.

16

Lawrence H. White

Privatization of Financial Sectors

The degree to which a modern economy's financial sector functions properly in large measure determines the economy's degree of success in real per capita growth and income over the long term. The financial sector plays two crucial roles. First, the financial system determines allocation of income between present and future (consumption today versus more consumption tomorrow through savings, investment, and capital formation) and allocation of current investment funds among various competing projects. Its second role is the administration of the payment system in the economy. Financial development—the emergence of sophisticated and efficient institutions for coordinating payments and investment decisions—has gone hand in hand with real per capita economic growth throughout economic history.[1]

The development of intermediary institutions fosters growth because it improves coordination between potential savers and investors, both nationally and internationally. It thereby increases the size of flows from savings into capital formation. Simultaneously and just as importantly, it improves the effectiveness of the process of allocation whereby investable funds are distributed among projects, increasing the useful capital-formation payoff from any given outlay of funds. Development of techniques of payment, which begins with monetization of the economy, allows increased coordination between specialist producers and potential buyers, expanding the possibilities for the division of labor.

Historical evidence indicates that financial institutions develop more strongly and efficiently when left to the private sector, primarily because the flexibility of private ownership promotes effective specialization among varieties of institutions. The profit motive channels financial entrepreneurs into the niches where their personal expertise operates most effectively to cultivate supplies of investable funds, to evaluate investment projects as worthy borrowers of funds, or to combine these two activities. The historical development of specialized financial market institutions in the economically advanced countries of the world — institutions such as stock and bond markets, brokerage houses, mutual funds, investment banks, and consumer banks — took place in a largely market-directed environment. This does not mean that an identical set of institutions is necessarily appropriate to developing countries today, or even constitutes a goal for the future. Different financial technologies are appropriate to different cultures, stages of development, and eras of history. The point is not the outcome of evolution elsewhere but the framework for the process: the private market framework allows the financial system to adapt itself best over time to the evolving desires of a developing society.

The chief social advantages of a market system of private and deregulated financial intermediaries over a nonmarket system of state-operated or state-controlled enterprises come from its use of market price signals and profit motive rather than arbitrary bureaucratic criteria to attract an appropriate volume of savings and to allocate the scarce pool of savings in society to its most productive uses. Market institutions can attract an appropriate volume of savings by establishing an interest rate paid to savers that accurately reflects the balance between perceived present and future wants in society. Interest is a reward paid for relinquishing present income in favor of future income. In developing countries where present wants are relatively urgent and where capital (the pool of resources for producing future income) is relatively scarce, high real interest rates will naturally prevail in the market. These attractive rates will persuade urban and rural income earners to provide adequate additions to the pool of capital in the economy. No compulsion or expropriation of income (from the agricultural sector to feed the industrial sector, for example) is necessary. Nor is it desirable if the process of growth is to respect the preferences of the public.

Unfortunately, state-owned financial institutions in developing countries have shown a tendency to try to suppress the knowledge that capital is scarce by holding interest rates below market-clearing figures. A shortage of loanable funds naturally arises as potential savings are inhibited while the demand to finance investment projects — especially capital-intensive and long-range projects — swells at artificially low rates of interest. Official credit must be rationed by some mechanism other than price. An unofficial market for funds springs up outside the banking sector, but intermediaries in this unsanctioned market typically cannot offer savers much security. Borrowers must therefore pay higher rates so that the intermediaries can offer the premium necessary to attract savings in the face of the risk of default. As a result, the imposition of an artificially low official interest rate, contrary to its ostensible aim, makes credit more expensive to all but a few borrowers.[2]

In private markets, the profit motive, guided by prices, effectively penalizes substandard performance in the allocation of loanable funds. The motive begins with individual savers, who seek the highest (risk-considered) yield. They will shift funds away from bankers who make too many loans to uncreditworthy borrowers or low-yield projects — and who consequently cannot pay much interest — toward better bankers who offer a higher yield on deposits. Bankers thus find that they must approve only those loans that give the best indication of genuine profitability (they are also subject to pressure exerted in this direction by their shareholders). The pursuit of profitability has the result (although it is not part of the banker's calculation) of steering loans toward projects with the highest potential for adding to aggregate wealth measured at market prices.[3] It also results in vesting responsibility for direction of resources in the most promising of a country's entrepreneurs. If banks and entrepreneurs are both guided by unmanipulated market prices, the investment projects selected will be appropriate to the country's wants and resource endowments as reflected in its relative prices for outputs and for labor, capital equipment, and raw materials. Unfortunately, many developing countries routinely manipulate the prices of consumer goods — through marketing boards, for example — and the prices of labor and capital goods. The continuation of nonmarket pricing policies in these areas would, of course, severely constrain the benefits of financial liberalization.

Conversely, elimination of price distortions would be highly complementary to privatization of the financial sector. Tax-funded government-sector financial institutions, in contrast to private banks, are not held continuously accountable for misallocations. They may continuously squander scarce social capital on loans that yield little or no return, and yet not be penalized by any reduction in the quantity of funds made available to them. In Bangladesh, for example, the repayment rate on loans from the government's development banks has been only 14 percent, with little or no penalty being placed on borrowers for loan delinquency.[4] Such "banks" are in practice making outright grants rather than loans. They are wasting scarce funds, and the real resources purchased with them, on projects that give no evidence of profitability. Because the recipients can nonetheless profit personally, scarce resources are also dissipated in lobbying efforts to obtain gratuitous loans. Where economic profitability is not a criterion, ample opportunity exists for favoritism in directing loans to politically well connected individuals, firms (particularly state-owned enterprises), industries, and regions. The same opportunity exists in a rationed credit market where government banks grant loans at below-market interest rates. The dreary spectacle of government favoritism and recipient lobbying is not, of course, unfamiliar to taxpayers in developed countries.

A third social advantage of private financial intermediaries is that they operate at lower cost, due to concern for their own profitability. State banks generally incur high overhead costs because of overstaffing and bureaucratization in addition to the large costs of writing off bad loans. Low rates of repayment sometimes prompt overmonitoring of loan recipients. A World Bank report on Indonesia estimated that its state banks' intermediation costs consumed 7 to 8 percentage points of interest rates charged.[5] Such a large wedge between loan rates and the rates payable to savers is a wasteful obstacle to intermediation. Long delays in service are another burden associated with state-run banking: loan decisions take an average of twelve months in Bangladesh,[6] and India's government-owned banks require five weeks to clear checks between Bombay and Calcutta.

Conditions

The privatization of the financial sector entails, first and foremost, transferring the assets of government-owned banks to the private sector. In a developing country the banking system typically dominates the financial sector, and in many cases provides practically the only formal market for intermediation (securities markets are generally of minor scope and importance). For a private banking system to thrive and make good use of assets, the following conditions are important:

Enforceable contract law. Lenders must be able to enforce collection of payments contractually due from borrowers. Borrowers must recognize that the failure of a project means the loss not only of borrowed funds but of pledged collateral, such as previously acquired equity. Government must not prevent the liquidation of insolvent firms.

Freedom from interest rate controls. Freedom of banks to set loan rates is crucial to the efficient placement of scarce loanable funds.[7] Complex interest rate structures that arbitrarily impose dozens of different lending rates for different classes of borrowers are particularly invidious. The Greek government, for example, sets one rate for small business and agricultural loans, one for long-term investment projects, one for working capital, and one for housing mortgages.[8] These rate structures, if they are at all binding, not only repress intermediation generally but also distort allocation by denying funds to sectors that are more productive at the margin than others. Freedom to set bank deposit rates, on the other side of the balance sheet, is crucial for bringing the savings of the nonwealthy out of hoarding, and perhaps even some of the savings of the wealthy elite back from overseas into the domestic financial system.

Open entry into banking. Transferring a highly concentrated banking system from government to private ownership may simply replace a state cartel with a nominally private cartel unless new entry is also permitted. Open entry is vital, and in banking (where cornering the market is a practical impossibility), generally sufficient for competitive pricing and other conditions to prevail. The optimal scale of banking firms and the individuals best suited to run them can be discovered only under these conditions.

Furthermore, with open entry, the most successful entrepreneurs in the informal financial sector of a developing economy—money-lenders, pawnbrokers, shopkeepers, middlemen—have the opportunity to develop and expand their traditional lending practices within banking structures as formal as they find appropriate. The most effective use can be made of their unique knowledge of local borrowers and circumstances. The transition from traditional to modern finance can be made most smoothly if traditional lenders are free to open formal banks. Native institutions that evolve in this way would seem to hold out the highest promise of mobilizing domestic savings economically and funneling them to the small rural and urban entrepreneurs who in many countries have been denied access to organized sources of financing.[9] Although it is independent of privatization, open entry for foreign banks is also desirable as an element of financial liberalization.

Nonregulation of bank portfolios. The following common political practices are for obvious reasons inimical to a thriving private banking industry: 1) forcing banks to hold stipulated quantities of government bonds or large quantities of central bank deposits; 2) requiring that certain proportions of bank assets be devoted to domestic investments or to specified classes of borrowers; 3) requiring bank borrowers to conform to arbitrary financial criteria. Privatization under rigid regulations such as these, or under conditions of discretionary official guidance along similar lines, is largely a mockery.

Types of Institutions

The privatization of banks potentially encompasses a number of types of institutions. Different types may call for different privatization strategies. We will focus on two broad groups.

State development and investment banks are not prime candidates for having their equity sold to private investors because their net worth is likely to be negative. "Recapitalizing" insolvent development banks would simply pour more taxpayer funds down the drain. The portfolios of such institutions can be privatized by selling their assets in secondary markets or by auction, to the extent that they consist of marketable forms, such as bonds and equity shares. Long-term loans to state enterprises that may themselves be in the process of being auctioned off can be converted into marketable bonds. Short-term loans, if any, may be allowed to run to maturity, at which point creditworthy borrowers can refinance with private bank loans. Costa Rica has begun the process of liquidating the portfolio of its insolvent state development bank. The brick-and-mortar capital of development banks is generally negligible, as by definition these banks do no consumer banking, so that finding new tenants should not be a major difficulty. This recommendation to liquidate state development banks is not intended to suggest that private development banks are impossible or undesirable; there are a number of examples to the contrary. But private development banks are probably better begun from scratch than from an attempt at radical conversion of an institution accustomed to continual tax infusions and considered more of a soft touch than a stern moneylender.

Consumer and commercial banks owned by government are more likely to be solvent, and therefore are candidates for privatization by an open auction of their equity. Bangladesh has denationalized two of its commercial banks by sale of equity to the public, with both sales being oversubscribed. Such a sale would naturally have to be preceded by an independent audit of balance sheet assets. One possible obstacle to straightforward application of this method arises when the scale of a state-owned banking enterprise is far too large for economical operation in its intended market (for example, the National Bank of Greece alone holds 60 percent of domestic bank deposits, almost nine times the sum held by its largest private competitor). The "optimal" scale of the new enterprise cannot be known in advance with much assurance. But it would seem reasonable to limit any newly privatized bank to an initial market share of 25 percent or less, so that at least four banks initially occupy the new market. Subsequent growth and mergers—which may be necessary to capture economies of larger scale — need not be discouraged. When entry is free, fears of monopoly power are unfounded. A well-planned division of assets both financial and physical will be necessary where a large state-owned bank is to be subdivided into two or more independent potential competitors.

Additional Steps

Privatizing the commercial and consumer banks that issue checking accounts is already an important step toward privatizing the payments mechanism. But there is a case for going at least two steps further, particularly for developing countries.

The first additional step is privatization of the international payments system; in other words, the foreign exchange market. This measure requires the elimination of the all-too-common system whereby the central bank fixes an official conversion rate of local to international currency but refuses to abide by it, pursuing instead an independent monetary policy. The central bank overexpands the stock of domestic currency and then refuses or finds itself unable to accommodate all demands to exchange local for foreign currency. By this strategy combined with credit controls, the central bank becomes a monopolist in a rationed foreign exchange market.

One alternative is a cleanly floating exchange rate. But for most developing economies this option is rendered infeasible by their smallness, specialized output, and resulting dependence on international trade and cross-border contracts. The other, more feasible alternative is monetary unification with one or more larger trading partners. In this arrangement, as practiced most consistently by Liberia and Panama, the monetary unit used domestically is one of the major internationally traded currency units, although it may carry a different local name. The advantages are straightforward: exchange risk is entirely eliminated for domestic and foreign firms trading within the unified currency area, and loans and investments from transnational banks and corporations are unobstructed by actual or feared exchange controls and the rationing of credit. Under complete monetary unification and financial liberalization, domestic banks can use foreign currency directly as reserves, accepting deposits and making loans denominated in that currency. The cost of monetary unification is sacrificing the opportunity for an independent national monetary policy. This is not a great loss and is probably a substantial gain for the citizens of most developing countries, whose monetary policies have brought high rates of inflation and have not been noticeably effective at dampening business cycles.

The second recommended step in privatization of payments consists of recognizing the right of private domestic banks to issue redeemable currency. The currency would be redeemable for central bank deposit liabilities or, if currency unification is undertaken, for widely accepted assets denominated in the internationally traded currency (such as actual pieces of a foreign currency). In the latter case the domestic central bank has no role whatsoever to play as a liability issuer. The interbank clearing system can be run by a private clearinghouse, as in Canada and many other developed nations. Systems of this kind proved successful in promoting the growth and industrialization of Scotland, the United States, Canada, and other Western nations in the last century before being shunted aside by central bank monopolization of currency issue. The primary advantage of a private bank currency system for a developing economy is that it sets the profit motive to work in promoting thorough monetization, which remains to be achieved in many developing areas. Competition for the profits from issuing currency leads banks to open branch agencies in comparatively remote areas, to provide services to customers and potential customers, and to otherwise encourage the use of money in place of barter.

Obstacles to Financial Privatization

The potential obstacles to a policy of privatizing state-owned financial institutions can be divided into two categories: interests and beliefs. Interests provoke the opposition of persons and agencies who fear a loss of power or income from the policy. Beliefs, mistaken or not, lead people and institutions not directly interested to support the status quo of state ownership.

The most obvious loss of income threatened by financial privatization is the central government's loss of revenue from "seigniorage," i.e., from printing new money and spending it into circulation. Where currency and bank reserves are privatized and the central bank is removed from the issue of high-powered money, the elimination of revenue from seigniorage is direct. But even a more modest policy of commercial bank privatization can, by making check payments a more attractive alternative to currency, reduce the real demand for and market value of central bank liabilities, and therefore indirectly reduce the real seigniorage income from any given rate of money creation. To overcome this obstacle, it will be necessary to convince governments either that substitute methods of raising revenue are preferable, or that spending should be reduced. The former is perhaps more likely, though the latter is possible.

A strong case can be made for the idea that high rates of monetary expansion are actually counterproductive as a means of raising revenue. First, they severely disrupt the organized economy so that activity in normally taxed channels (such as imports, exports, production, and sales) is constricted, bringing down tax yields. The economy is depressed below its potential volume of output, and a larger share of the remaining activity is diverted into informal channels (such as barter) that are difficult to tax. Second, at the high rates of price inflation accompanying rapid monetary expansion, increases in nominal tax receipts tend to lag behind increases in prices, so that real (inflation-adjusted) tax receipts shrink. In several Latin American nations this shrinkage has been found to be dramatic. When a government attempts to make up its revenue shortfall by stepping up monetary expansion even higher, the economy is headed toward a hyperinflation crack-up. Forswearing inflationary finance by privatizing the issuing of money is a credible method of keeping the economy from going down that path.

The income and prestige of officials in state-run development banks and other institutions are naturally threatened by privatization. It can be pointed out to such officials that the opportunity to administer private banks will reward them more lucratively. If they demur, they admit that they are not really skilled at evaluating the profitability of projects proposed by borrowers. But the real obstacle is that these officials are in fact likely to be skilled at cultivating constituencies of favored borrowers. These constituencies may be highly organized. They know the game of wrangling loans from the state banks on concessionary terms, but may fear strongly—and often for good reason—

that private banks will be less accommodating. The larger number of entrepreneurs and members of the public who will benefit from an open and competitive loan market may not be easy for anyone to identify before privatization. In countries that have successfully liberalized their financial sectors (such as Indonesia and South Korea), it has been necessary to form a broad-based consensus that the change will be good for all, however much inconvenience it may cause for some in the short run.

The beliefs inimical to privatization held by those not pecuniarily interested are sometimes outgrowths of a lack of appreciation for the virtues of decentralized markets; that is, for letting individuals make decisions for themselves. In the financial sector the principal fear seems to be that private banks will not choose to make the "right" sorts of loans. But private banks have every incentive to seek out and make loans to projects that look to be profitable — projects that promise to add to total wealth — since these are the ones to combine relatively low valued resources into higher-valued products. It is difficult to see what is "wrong" about this criterion.

It might be argued that the judgments of banks concerning the profitability of various investment projects do not incorporate the social benefits of the projects (their valued spillover effects) and that government therefore has a role to play in providing subsidized loans to deserving areas of the economy neglected by the private financial system. But what are these supposed social benefits? One development economics text accounts for subsidized loans to heavy industry by noting that "it is industrial development that is expected [by governments] to bring desired employment opportunities and technological advances to complement local programmes of education and generally to conform with the aspirations of development plans."[10] In some developing countries, agriculture is expected to bring such benefits. The benefits, in other words, consist of twisting the economy in a direction preferred by central planners or the politically favored, not of producing effects generally valued by members of the public. The "desired employment opportunities" for some come at the expense of denied opportunities for many in the sectors passed over by the political allocation of loans. Even if there were valid arguments for subsidization of some projects (and criticism of the argument for subsidy based on the notion of social benefits or positive externality is obviously beyond the scope of this discussion), the mixing of subsidy decisions with bona fide loan decisions in state development banks is a recipe for contaminating the lending process with grant seeking, with all the disadvantageous consequences that can readily be predicted.

Extreme skepticism is likewise warranted toward assertions that private banks will make too few loans to projects that are small in scale, high in risk, or located in certain areas. If these projects appear at least to some banks to be profitable for loans (and at an interest rate that incorporates an appropriate risk premium they should so appear), it is hard to see why all banks would shun them. If they do not appear to any bank to be profitable, it is difficult to understand why it would be improper for the banks to shun them. There is no obvious reason for believing that any projects are entitled to subsidy simply by virtue of their small scale, high risk, or location.

A certain diffidence toward privatization is understandably shown by people who regard it as a process for handing state-owned enterprises over to nominally private associates of authoritarian rulers, citing the Philippines under Marcos and Brazil as examples of such a process. No oligarchic policy of this sort is being advocated or excused here. Privatization of the financial sector is instead proposed as part of the agenda for genuine liberalization, decentralization, and separation of economic affairs from political power.

17
Steve H. Hanke

The Anatomy of a Successful Debt Swap

Debt swaps have been endorsed by the Reagan Administration as part of the so-called Baker Plan, by various multi-national lending organizations, and by independent students of international finance. The swaps are a means of reducing external debt and of stimulating the flow of capital to indebted nations. Since this flow of external capital can, among other things, provide a source of financing for newly privatized enterprises, debt swaps can play an important role in promoting privatization, particularly in countries where domestic savings rates are low.

Debt swaps come in two generic forms: The first, most widely recognized type involves the conversion of external debt denominated in a foreign currency into internal equity denominated in a home country's currency. The second type involves the conversion of external debt denominated in a foreign currency into internal debt denominated in a home country's currency.

Although discussions have generated enthusiasm for debt swaps, the only country that has been able to make good use of them is Chile. Since they were introduced in 1985, swaps have equaled almost 10 percent of Chile's outstanding debt to foreign commercial banks. Why has the Chilean debt swap program been successful in reducing that country's external debt, stimulating the flow of capital to Chile, and in part, financing that country's privatizations? This chapter addresses these questions.

The Rationale For International Investing

One necessary condition for a successful debt swap program is the availability of attractive investment opportunities in the country that institutes a swap program. If there are no attractive investment possibilities, there will be no demand for debt swaps, regardless of how well the program is designed. However, attractive investment opportunities do not constitute a sufficient condition for a successful swap program. Even if there are attractive investment opportunities, investors might choose not to use swaps, if the swap program is poorly designed. International investing is most attractive when it promises opportunities for 1) portfolio diversification, 2) good values and 3) attractive returns.

Those who are averse to risk attempt to diversify their investment portfolios so that risk can be reduced. To diversify prudently does not mean that one indiscriminately spreads investments around. Rather, one should pick investments so that the total return on a portfolio is correlated to the return in the market in general. In the United States, for example, this can be done by holding approximately thirty stocks whose returns tend to be unrelated (or dissimilar) to each other but, when taken together, generate a total return that is highly correlated to the market return. This type of diversity tends to eliminate risk within a market because the returns on a portfolio parallel those of the entire market. While risk can be diversified, a portfolio will still contain risk associated with the market in general. The only way to lower this so-called market risk — the risk associated with having a well diversified "market portfolio" fully invested in one market — is to expand the definition of the market to include other markets. As good diversifiers, these other markets should generate returns that are unrelated (or dissimilar) to those in the original market. This is where international markets come into play. The exchange in Santiago, Chile, the Bolsa de Valores, provides us with an excellent diversifier of market risk because the pattern of its returns is essentially unrelated to that generated in the United States. For example, using annual data from 1975–86, the correlation coefficient between the index for shares traded on the Bolsa de Valores and the Standard and Poor's 500 index was − 0.09.[1] Given the relationship between returns in the Chilean market and those in the United States, one is able — by expanding "the market" to include Chile — to reduce the risk associated with being fully invested in the United States. Or, to put it another way, the increased diversity gained by investing a portion of a portfolio in Chile allows one to earn higher returns per unit of risk than one would with a well-diversified, all-American portfolio.

In addition to the Chilean market's attractiveness from an overall diversification point of view, it also offers an opportunity to purchase shares that are good values. For example, the average price-earnings ratio for shares on the Bolsa de Valores is about 7.0, whereas the same ratio for the Standard and Poor's 500 shares is about 18.0. In addition, the Chilean market's shares are selling at a discount to their book value. The Chilean market is also attractive because it promises high rates of return. For example, from 1975 to 1986 an index based on the Standard and Poor's 500 stocks increased from 100 to 449; and during the same period the Morgan Stanley World Index of stocks rose from 100 to 567. The index for the shares traded on the Santiago's Bolsa de Valores, however, increased from 100 to 2,060 during the same period. This represents one of the best records for stock returns in the world.

There is no better indicator of a nation's economic well-being than the confidence (or lack thereof) its own investors show by how and where they spend their money. Flight capital is perhaps the best foul-weather barometer for any nation's economy. This is particularly the case for Latin America, where flight capital has become endemic. Chile is the one Latin nation in which the flight capital phenomenon has been clearly reversed; Chileans have actually been repatriating capital and earnings from abroad. For example, in 1985–86, about $1.4 billion worth of flight capital returned to Chile. This is equal to about 10 percent of that country's debt to foreign commercial banks. The underlying reason for this return of flight capital is the lure of high, risk-adjusted rates of return at home.

The prospect of significant, risk-adjusted rates of return is the necessary condition to arrest and reverse the flight of capital. Chile has met this necessary condition by implementing sweeping privatizations. This has strengthened the role of private ownership and market forces in the economy. Since 1974, Corfo, the state industrial promotion corporation, has received about $1.3 billion from the sales of state-owned enterprises. These sales have included CAP, a steel and iron ore producer (100 percent privatized); ChilMetro, an electricity distribution firm (100 percent privatized), ChilQuinta, an electricity distribution firm (100 percent privatized); Soquimich, a nitrate producer (65 percent privatized); LabChile, a producer of pharmaceuticals and chemicals (49 percent privatized); Enacar, a coal producer (49 percent privatized); ChilGener, a generator of electricity (49 percent privatized); Iansa, a sugar refinery (46 percent privatized); and Entel, a telecommunications firm (33 percent privatized). Additional privatizations have been authorized, including electric generation firms, another coal producer, and LanChile, Chile's nationalized airline.

Noteworthy in Chile's program to promote free enterprise is its privatized social security system. On November 4, 1980 eligible workers were given the option of staying with the public social security system or moving to private social security. To date, over 90 percent of these workers have enrolled in private pension funds. The domestic savings generated by private social security have, in part, been used to purchase shares in newly privatized enterprises. The private pensions are acting like a chemotherapeutic treatment that is eating away at the cancer of nationalized enterprises. It is interesting to note that the controlling interest in Provida, Chile's largest private pension fund manager, was acquired in early 1986 by Bankers Trust in New York through a $43 million debt-for-equity swap.

Employee stock-ownership plans (ESOPs) are an integral part of Chile's "Popular Capitalism" program, and have become quite popular. For example, when the steel company (CAP) was privatized, one-third of the shares were purchased by employees, with 4,000 of the

6,500 employees participating in the ESOPs plan. In late 1985, the government sold a computer services firm, ECOM. In this case, the union, which represented all the firm's employees, recommended that its members purchase ECOM's shares. In consequence, 114 of the 120 employees participated in the $1.5 million sale. They financed their purchases with a ten-year loan from the government's industrial promotion corporation, Corfo.

Privatizations, with ownership diffusion generated through the private social security system and ESOPs, have increased the depth and width of the Chilean capital market. Moreover, they have increased the popularity of owning shares. Chile has complemented that program by reducing economic distortions associated with high tariffs, subsidies, and taxes. Moreover, it has followed prudent monetary policies that have kept its inflation rates low by Latin standards. In consequence, real growth was almost 6 percent in 1986, unemployment ended the year slightly under 9 percent, and the country's trade surplus continued to grow.

Chile's Debt Swap Program

Building on its attractive investment climate, Chile allowed for an acceleration in the flow of external capital into the country when it changed its foreign-exchange regulations in 1985. These changes permit the conversion of external-debt obligations owed by Chileans into Chilean peso obligations. That such conversions are attractive is revealed by the markets. At the time of this writing, participants in the secondary market for external Chilean debt value it at about 67 percent of face value. When it is converted into pesos, its value in the Chilean capital market increases to about 92 percent of face value. To capitalize on this possibility for intermarket arbitrage, two new chapters were added to the Banco Central's "Compendium of Rules for International Exchange." Chapter XIX allows for the exchange of foreign debt for local equity. This is aimed at foreign investors who wish to purchase external Chilean debt for the purpose of capitalizing it into investments in Chile. The debt-for-equity swaps that are made possible under Chapter XIX, have received a good bit of attention because they are similar to swaps being conducted in Argentina, Brazil, and Mexico, and because they have also acted to increase the flow of foreign investment into Chile and strengthen the economy.

Even though international attention has been focused on Chapter XIX swaps, only about 40 percent of Chile's 1986 swaps were implemented under this provision. The largest of these was completed by Carter Holt Harvey, a New Zealand forest products company. It purchased almost half of Copec, the largest private company in Chile and the owner of Celulosa Arauco y Constitucion, Chile's leading pulp producer. Fletcher Challenge, another New Zealand firm, is in the final stages of an even larger Chapter XIX swap that will facilitate its purchase of 79,000 acres of Chilean timberland.

The new Chapter XVIII, which is uniquely Chilean, accounted from about 60 percent of the 1986 swaps. However, Chapter XVIII has received virtually no attention outside Chile. It is this chapter that provides the key to understanding why Chileans have accelerated the repatriation of capital they hold abroad. Chapter XVIII is specifically aimed at Chilean investors. It permits Chileans to use their assets abroad to purchase external debt and convert it into domestic debt. This allows for an arbitrage profit on repatriated flight capital, which adds to the yields on investments made with these funds. It therefore increases the likelihood that Chilean-owned funds held abroad, which are estimated at $2 to $3 billion, will be pulled back into Chile.

The external-for-internal debt swaps work in this manner: a Chilean investor, through a foreign agent, locates Chilean foreign debt that qualifies for prepayment and redenomination into pesos. After locating the external debt which can be purchased at a discount of about 33 percent of face value, the Chilean investor authorizes a Chilean bank to obtain the agreement of the affected Chilean debtor to have the foreign debt redenominated into pesos at par based on the official exchange rate. The Chilean bank then submits a sealed bid for a ration coupon to the Banco Central. This bid indicates how much the Chilean investor will pay the Banco Central for the right to have the external debt converted into an internal one. The reason for the ration coupons is central to understanding why the debt conversions work.

If the total amount of conversions were left uncontrolled, these transactions could add to Chile's money supply and create inflation.

They could also cause the value of the peso in the parallel (free) market to become increasingly devalued relative to the official peso rate. In consequence of these considerations, the Banco Central has managed the impact of these conversions by setting a monthly quota (ration coupons) for the total amount of conversions allowed. This allocation is rationed to Chilean investors on the basis of their coupon bids. The Banco Central has been able to prudently manage the total allocations, so that it can "sterilize" the effect of the conversions on the Chilean money supply and keep the parallel rate close enough to the official one to guarantee profits from conversions.[2]

Once approved, the purchase of the foreign debt is made, through the Chilean investor's foreign agent, and delivered to the Chilean bank. The Chilean bank redenominates the external debt into pesos and creates a new, internal peso debt instrument. It is at this point that the foreign debt is canceled and the new indexed instrument, which requires the Chilean debtor to pay the bearer a single payment in fifteen years, is delivered to a Chilean agent. Since the new, local instrument is indexed to Chilean inflation — so that the real yield is fixed — the final payment can't be determined until the new instrument is due.

Finally, the Chilean agent places the new peso-denominated debt in the local capital market and receives about 92 percent of par. These receipts are then delivered to the Chilean investor. It is important to mention that, contrary to debt conversions in Argentina, Brazil, and Mexico, where the central banks place the value on external debt conversions, it is the capital market in Chile that performs this task and creates the possibility for intermarket arbitrage. This represents yet another indicator of Chile's commitment to free markets. The Chileans have, in contrast to other Latin countries, a well-developed, liquid-capital market in which long-term debt instruments are actively traded. The Chileans have chosen to allow the debt-valuation and conversion work to be done by the participants in this open market, rather than by bureaucrats at a central bank. It is also important to mention that the capital market is large enough to allow the Banco Central to effectively "sterilize" a rather large volume of swaps; for example, the swaps have been running at roughly 10 percent of the monetary base each month.

For the foreign investors who must use Chapter XIX, the process for implementing a swap is exactly the same as that used by a Chilean who uses Chapter XVIII, with one exception. Foreign investors do not have to pay the Banco Central for the right to make a debt swap. This, of course, means that intermarket arbitrage profits are larger for swaps initiated by foreigners than by Chileans. After foreign investors receive Chilean pesos from a swap, investments can be made in Chile. After a four-year period, investors are free to repatriate 25 percent of past dividends, and all future dividends. After 10 years, they can repatriate their entire capital.

Conclusion

Debt swaps can be succesful if the countries that institute them provide investors with attractive places to park their capital. Chile's debt swap program has been successful because it offers such a parking place. It provides investors with excellent opportunities for portfolio diversification, good investment values, and high returns. Investors who have been attracted to the Chilean market have used the swap mechanism because it is free-market in its design and because by using it they can obtain Chilean pesos at a discount, which is equal to the arbitrage profit generated by the swap. Chile has demonstrated that a well-functioning debt swap program can provide a significant source of finance for privatization, and that this stimulation can fuel an accelerating privatization program.

18

Madsen Pirie and Peter Young

Development with Aid:
Public and Private Responsibilities
in Privatization

The major problem in the Third World is the lack of adequate capital markets. But experience shows that giving money alone to the governments of less-developed countries (LDCs) is questionable. Financial aid to developing countries should to a greater extent be made conditional on their economic policies, particularly on their progress toward privatization. When aid is given for development projects, private sector involvement should be urged, and where possible made a condition of aid. For example, aid to construct and operate irrigation networks, roads, or electricity generation facilities should be given on the condition that these be privately built and operated.

Obviously, the experience of developed countries does not translate verbatim to the Third World. Nevertheless, important lessons can be learned, including the following:

- Units should be established within development agencies and given responsibility specifically to encourage privatization in the developing world. The units should coordinate policies to promote privatization, including the policies of other government departments and agencies.

- Specialist teams are needed to provide advice to developing countries. These teams should be made up of officials with privatization experience from government departments and agencies, managers laid off from newly privatized companies, and experienced individuals seconded from financial institutions with privatization expertise.

- Regular conferences should be held in Asia, Africa, and Latin America at which specialists from the developed and developing world outline their views and experience of privatization and assess Third World problems and perspectives. As Third World experience with privatization grows, it should be subject to constant review. The production of a series of how-to privatization manuals is a good idea.

- Representatives of Western governments should take a more active role in advocating privatization when visiting other countries. In particular, government representatives responsible for trade matters, who travel more regularly than other ministers, could point out more aggressively the benefits of privatization for increased economic activity and trade.

- Funding should be provided for delegations of LDC officials to visit Britain and other countries having an extensive privatization record to gather information. LDC officials should be apprenticed to Western government departments actively involved in privatization.

A variety of new policies and initiatives would thus be required to form the basis of a comprehensive program to boost privatization and economic growth in the Third World. The initiatives we propose can be broken down into two types: financial assistance, and information and advice.

Financial Assistance

Because most developing countries lack the capital markets for Western-style privatization, the successes of the United Kingdom are not easily transplanted to them. However, there is much the developed countries can do to remedy the problem of lack of capital. Indeed, privatization itself could prove an important means of building up capital ownership in developing countries and thus spurring further economic growth. This should be an aim of privatization, and policies should be crafted to help achieve it.

An additional problem in many developing countries is antipathy to foreign ownership. This is a legacy of the colonial period, when LDC economies were largely controlled by Western interests. Indeed, the desire for domestic ownership of industries was a key factor in the nationalization of many LDC enterprises. Thus the takeover of nationalized concerns by foreign interests is not a popular option in most of these countries.

Concerns about capital and foreign ownership can be appeased through contracting out, by which the LDC government remains in charge of the government function, but contracts out its operations to qualified firms. Companies specialize in providing such services as garbage collection, street cleaning, and air traffic control to LDC governments. This practice should be encouraged and expanded because it saves money, allows scarce resources to be spent elsewhere, and builds indigenous private sector expertise in the provision of the contracted services. Western firms under contract in LDCs usually employ indigenous managers who can gain the experience to start their own contracting firms. Development policy should foster contracting out by offering advice about writing contracts. It should encourage firms to employ indigenous personnel, train them to form their own contracting companies, and lend them start-up funds.

Foreign capital can be attracted through the creation of free zones or free ports in LDCs without many of the common political problems. LDCs should be given advice and financial assistance to set these up. Free zones can act as a focus for investment and as a location for private companies, which can provide capital for privatization. They are already proving to be a useful innovation in the developing world, and their number has increased dramatically in recent years. The provision of tax incentives by developed countries for their companies investing in these zones might also be a useful policy.

To make a state operation profitable and suitable for privatization, money may have to be invested in it. Western countries can provide the investment capital needed to enable LDCs to bring state operations up to the level where they can be considered privatization candidates. For example, unemployment of public and agency employees in the wake of privatization is a major problem with potentially significant political consequences. One method of dealing with the problem is to provide layoff payments to staff members substantial enough for the transition to a new job or start-up of a business. LDC governments lacking the resources to do this may incur severe political hostility from the displaced staff, mitigating the viability of privatization. In these circumstances development agencies should consider making funds available to LDC governments for layoff payments. Although the money goes to people in the form of severance pay and cash sums for pensions, it is nonetheless capital investment: money is being put up in order to secure a more profitable and efficient future.

This technique is also useful to get full support for a privatization effort. If a company is failing badly, accruing great losses, those involved in the process — including the public — may be fearful that a sale to the private sector will result in the stripping of the operation's assets, resulting in a large number of jobs lost, as well as the service itself. Of course, it may be that the best thing is for the operation to be abandoned. But every effort should first be made to make the enterprise viable. Following that, every effort must be made to transfer the enterprise to the private sector — tax concessions, transitional arrangements, extended payments, interest-free loans — whatever it takes. Once it is in the private sector, these preparations will make it much easier to make the enterprise economically viable. This, in turn, will make privatization more popular. It must constantly be stressed that privatization is a process of political economy, not just of economics.

Increased measures are required to surmount the problem of lack of capital. Free distribution of stocks to the indigenous population would ensure broad-based capital ownership, but presents some practical difficulties. The policy has been advocated by a number of commentators — notably Dr. David Owen, leader of the British Social

Democratic Party, and Samuel Brittan, deputy editor of the *Financial Times* of London—but it has rarely been implemented. A successful free distribution of stock did occur in British Columbia, where shares in the British Columbia Resources Investment Corporation (BCRIC) were distributed to all members of the population who applied for them. A remarkable 86 percent did so, and a brisk market in the stocks soon developed. The only fair method of share allocation is among the entire population. In large LDCs this could result in stocks of very little value being given to very many people, but this problem can be overcome by putting the assets of a number of state concerns into a holding company for distribution. The policy is generally more suitable for smaller LDCs.

A more attractive variation of this policy would be for the development agencies to buy a portion of the stocks at the market rate, then put them on sale to the population at one half or one third the market rate. In order to achieve the objective of broad-based stock ownership and prevent stocks from being snapped up by a few rich individuals or institutions, limits should be placed on the amount of stock that one person or institution can buy.

This method of sale is similar to that used in the privatization of British Telecom. Stocks were put on the market well below their market price, as was evidenced by the fact that the value of the stock doubled on the first day of trading, and strict limits were placed on the number that could be purchased by any one individual. More than 2 million people bought stocks, most of them for the first time. An important component of the success of this privatization was a very large advertising campaign to educate members of the public about the stock offer. Such a campaign would be even more important in LDCs, and development agencies might advise on how this should be carried out, and provide some of the funds required to pay for it.

An even more appropriate privatization model might be that of the employee takeover or buy-out. Here we have some British experience that is more applicable to LDCs than is conventional privatization. In these cases ownership is transferred to people with little wealth or knowledge of stock markets. This form of privatization has proved uniformly popular with the employees of state-owned concerns and is thus politically attractive.

In some LDCs development agencies can help train management and employees to mount buy-outs, educate workers about stocks, provide loan facilities for workers to buy stocks and repay the loans through their wage packets, and lend the bulk of the funds required to finance the purchase of the concern from the government. Another possibility is for the development agency to carry out the policy itself, then compensate the government for the funds lost in selling below the market price. Such an agreement would result in development agencies having less influence over the privatization attempt, but might prevent political complications resulting from direct participation in the sale.

Information and Advice

It would be wise for Western governments to step as far back as possible from the actual implementation of privatization, leaving the decision of whether and how to go about it to the Third World governments involved. However, stimulated by Western governments and welcomed by LDC governments, the private sector in the West can perform a growing role in encouraging privatization in developing countries. Western investment banks, accounting firms, and advertising agencies have much experience in handling privatizations and can apply their expertise to LDC privatizations. Western investment banks can handle stock issues and do the underwriting. Management consulting and accounting firms can help prepare state enterprises for privatization, and advertising agencies should conduct the publicity campaigns necessary to interest the LDC public in buying stock. Some Western firms are already active in this field and do not need much encouragement to increase their commitment. Private Western investment in privatized LDC companies should be encouraged by the creation of appropriate tax advantages, especially ones that apply to mutual funds specializing in LDC privatized equity. However, foreign ownership of private companies in the Third World should be avoided, since that was the reason many companies were nationalized in the first place.

The creation of capital pools to promote Third World privatization would be a very useful policy innovation. The pools could be used to find and develop profitable privatization opportunities in developing countries. Tax advantages (perhaps a shelter from some capital taxes) are justified both on the grounds of the social benefit their activities will bring and by the high-risk nature of the investments. The private sector should be encouraged to lend against equity held by investors in privatized Third World companies. In other words, equity in such companies should be regarded as security for a loan, enabling LDC entrepreneurs to commit their funds to privatization projects but retain liquidity.

Governments might encourage this practice by acting as secondary guarantor. Banks should be encouraged to convert part of the debt owed by LDCs into equity; Western governments might provide incentives. LDC governments can reduce their debt burden and interest payments by swapping debt for equity in companies being privatized. Stock given to the banks can have conditions attached, such as resale to indigenous investors within ten years. Such a policy also commits Western banks to ensuring the success and profitability of the companies concerned. Financial institutions should be encouraged to provide facilities that enable LDC investors to buy stock in privatized companies on credit. Such facilities were provided to investors in British Telecom when it was privatized; the investors were allowed to pay for their stock in three installments over a period of eighteen months.

LDC Governments

The most important role for LDC governments in promoting privatization is in creating an appropriate investment climate. This means guaranteeing property and contract rights and maintaining an impartial system of adjudication for property disputes. Investors must be free from the fear of government expropriation. The rule of law must regulate transactions, with the conviction that government itself respects that rule.

Tax structures must not militate against achievement and success, but should allow people to garner and retain the rewards of taking risks and engaging in enterprise. Tax rates must be low on corporate as well as personal incomes, and such tax burden as is necessary should fall more heavily on consumption than on sources of investment.

Capital must be able to move within and out of the country. Foreign investors are attracted by capital they can recover as well as invest in. Free trade must be permitted, without tariff barriers to regulate or preselect the types of activity that may take place. There is a need to discover and exploit comparative advantage rather than attempt to produce behind tariff walls what can already be produced more cheaply elsewhere.

Above all, LDCs must have a proper understanding of privatization as a creative process designed to shift whole areas of economic activity, with their attendant interest groups, from the politicized, noncommercial state sector to the consumer-responsive, profit-making private sector. Privatization should not be just a means of raising funds quickly by selling off a few state assets, nor a means of granting favors to a handful of individuals or companies by allowing them to buy such assets at low prices. It should involve as many people as possible in the creation of wealth.

A final task for LDC governments is to prevent mismanagement and favoritism in contracting out by establishing a respected competitive bidding process. It would be wise to set up an independent board of respected figures to decide which services should be contracted out and to oversee the tendering process.

The LDC Private Sector

The most important role that the private sector can play is to show interest in potential privatizations and to put forward bids. Governments need to determine that there is a reasonable level of interest in the privatization of a particular concern before the process is begun. Private companies, trade associations, and chambers of commerce should conduct reviews of the public sector and suggest which entities could be put into private hands and which interests would like to invest in them. The private sector should also help create a climate of confidence for privatization in which the government itself believes it can privatize without the embarrassment of failure.

Conclusion

Some of the policy options mentioned here are complementary; others are alternatives. The balance among the roles played by Western development agencies, the private sector in the West, and LDC governments will vary. Western governmental agencies should attempt to keep their role to a minimum: they should stimulate the desired policy change, but leave as much of the work as possible to the private sector and LDC governments. For example, Western governments should take a secondary role rather than be a primary lender, and provide seed capital to start a privatization project rather than finance it all. The extent of their involvement will vary from country to country; and as private sector and LDC expertise in privatization builds up, Western governments will be able to reduce their own commitments.

Part V

Cases of Privatization

19

John Redwood

Privatization:
The Case of Britain

Privatization in the United Kingdom began a long time ago. It used to be called denationalization, and it was a game of Ping-Pong played between the socialist and conservative parties. For thirty years the most common ball in the game has been the British steel industry. First the socialist party would nationalize it; then the conservative party would rescue it from the evil clutches of the public sector, only to lose a subsequent election and see it fall back again. These origins of privatization, funny though they may be, are also important, because sometimes the enthusiasm and vested interests needed for a successful privatization program come *ab initio* from those enterprises that have most recently been nationalized, and where there is an atmosphere of greater sympathy for returning them to their "rightful home," the private sector.

In the early 1970s there was a chance to go further. By surprise, the Conservative government of Edward Heath was elected, and he was committed to free-market economics. When Heath took office, he saw to it that several drinking establishments in Carlisle were returned to the private sector — a good English place to begin privatization, you might say. A travel agency was also moved over. But by 1972 the combined might and intelligence of the British civil service brought the program to a grinding halt, enveloping Mr. Heath in the largest program of peacetime controls on the economy that our country has seen — and I hope ever will see. He was busy legislating for price controls and earnings controls and wage controls and dividend controls, and in that climate, of course, there was not much scope for privatization. Indeed, there was not much scope for business at all.

Mr. Heath was soon dismissed from office, and the civil service had claimed another scalp for their collection. Be warned, those of you who set out on privatization. Do not listen to the doubters and better-notters and do-notters, because they will bring your government down just as truly as Mr. Heath's was brought down by evil advice from evil counselors.

Between 1974 and 1979, our Conservative Party was able to piece together its intellectual heritage and rebuild its forces in favor of liberal economics, market and price forces, and, of course, privatization. When the party was returned to power in 1979, the program of privatization began slowly, timorously, gently. There was the sale of some shares in British Petroleum, but it was already a quoted company and they were easy to sell. The sale raised some much-needed money, but there wasn't much more to it than that; indeed the Labour government had been forced into selling them some years earlier on one of its regular trips to the International Monetary Fund to borrow money.

So, too, did the new government begin the task of reversing the most recent nationalizations of the Labour government. But one of them proved very difficult. The shipbuilding industry, which had been brought into the public sector, had arrived just in time for the biggest slump in shipbuilding orders the world has ever seen. By the time the Conservative government came in, it was operating at a heavy loss, and all the debate centered around how much should be done within the public sector before it could be transformed again. But that was not true of the aerospace industries that had also been brought into public ownership, and they were quickly dispatched back to the private sector. However, their original owners were not so keen to buy them back as we thought at first, so they were eventually sold as a package of assets in the form of a new public corporation, British Aerospace.

By 1981 to 1982, it was still not clear whether the privatization movement was going to gather momentum or amount to a little bit of ideology and a little bit of money raising. At this stage, public support was frankly not good. Conservative popularity had slumped in the polls. There was no body of opinion within the country beyond the confines of the Conservative Party in favor of privatization. We had failed in our central task: to convince the people that life would be better if competition were introduced. We simply had not won the preparatory intellectual skirmish and were not confident that we could go on to a major program; so the program puttered on.

Amersham, a small radiochemical company that ran quite well, was privatized; then Cable & Wireless, a large international telecommunications company that was keen on getting into the private sector because it was finding onerous the controls placed by the Treasury on its overseas investment and expansion plans. Management was enthusiastic, which is a large part of the battle. Sometimes management naturally wants to fly to the private sector. Other times it doesn't like the choices it is offered if it stays in the public sector. There was a shipbuilding yard specializing in building rigs for the North Sea in Scot Lithgow, Scotland, whose choice was very simple. The nationalized British shipbuilders' industry was going to close the yard because it could see no way of stopping the losses or saving the jobs. We decided to give the private sector a chance. The new owners named a high price for taking it, but we decided it would be better to give the work force and management a chance under a new company with proven management skills. When they were offered the choice, the employees were keen to take it. The yard is still going and is much more productive than when closure loomed.

The government paid out money in that privatization. Negative bids have to be allowed if you have a very bad asset. Otherwise there are the enormous costs of closure, which can exceed the negative bid, or there are losses year after year. Some of the best deals have been ones in which no money at all was raised, or where it was actually paid out.

British Telecom

The important decision — the one that foretold that this privatization movement was going to be different in kind, tempo, and excitement from all the previous ones — was the decision made by Sir Keith Joseph, Industry Minister, after much consideration, to privatize British Telecom. His advisors argued that the industry should be opened to competition, as a market test for the services it provided and the prices it charged.

At the time, his decision was derided. We were told there was no chance of selling an organization as large as British Telecom, as £2 billion to 4 billion might be needed from investors in a stock market that had never before managed more than 300 or 400 million. We were told there was no chance of improving service, cutting prices, or improving the performance of the organization by introducing competition. We were told that it was a state monopoly and would always remain so, and that in any case its service was good. Waiting six months for a new phone was considered adequate, as was the choice of just two kinds of phone at the prices set by British Telecom.

Our policy of introducing competition into this utility began to win friends as individuals saw that liberalization and eventually a change of ownership could bring improvement. Suddenly, forty or fifty different types of phones would be available, either through purchase or rental. The price of intercity phone calls would fall by as much as 30 percent on lines open to competition. And tariff increases, now under a new regulatory price system, would be much lower than the general rate of inflation, where before they were nearly always higher.

These tangible customer benefits helped build a base of political interest in favor of the whole process. The scale of the program is now large. In the first year only some of £370 million of assets were sold, about $500 million, in an economy with a gross national product of £300 billion. As of last year, the total since 1979 hit £8 billion of assets sold, or about $11 billion. In a single year, from March 1986 to March 1987, the government will sell £4.75 billion of assets, and it will go on to sell much more.

Starting with 10 percent of the industrial and trading economy in state hands, by the end of Margaret Thatcher's second administration we were down to half that, and there is no reason why we can't complete the process in her third term. We have devolved powers to local government, and some of the largest councils are not governed by the same part or interest as governs the nation as a whole. This split of powers is healthy, but it does affect what you can do. The policy we've adopted is to encourage or even legislate to ensure that some kinds of local government service are put out to competitive tender.

Themes

Themes that have helped us to win public opinion countrywide include the idea that more individuals should participate in the industrial and commercial wealth of the nation by buying and owning shares. British Telecom was the important change. In a single issue, 2 million citizens bought shares in their telephone company. To date, 1.75 million of them remain shareholders, although we were told at the time that it would be a two-day wonder, that they would all sell out to the big institutions. They are still there because there is a genuine thirst for ownership, and pleasure in owning an asset that is a part of their lives.

Another equally important theme is bringing the employees into the process of management, ownership, and profit sharing. The greatest success — and in some ways the connoisseur's choice of U.K. privatizations — was the National Freight Corporation. This was a badly managed lorry business, the largest over-the-road hauler in the United Kingdom, which had rarely made a profit. The Minister of Transport persuaded the drivers and managers to buy the company for themselves. We sold it for £50 million. Practically all that money was needed to sort out the pension fund and other liabilities.

But that didn't matter. What mattered was that the lorry drivers and managers acquired assets that had rarely made money, and transformed the company into a proud one providing first-class service. Profits soared. The shareholders who got in on the ground floor are, four years later, sitting on an 11.5-fold increase in the value of their shares, and profits are still rising.

Opponents insisted that the employees would not be able to make the hard decisions needed. But at a 1986 meeting of the company to which more than half of the employees were entitled to come and vote as shareholders, some interesting things transpired. First, they voted to invest some of their profits overseas — although unions are always against this in the United Kingdom — because they thought there were good opportunities for investment. Second, they voted down a proposal to have special worker directors on the board, on the grounds that they could elect the whole board as shareholders, and that they would rather have people on the board who knew what they were doing. And third, they made a decision to lay off some employees because one part of the business wasn't profitable: they agreed that the money saved would be invested elsewhere in the business to guarantee its future prosperity.

Another important theme in creating a marketplace for privatization politically and economically has been the better performance that comes from a privatized business. We have few exceptions to the rule that, once privatized, a business finds its profits go up. We have few exceptions to the rule that they invest more and are freer to decide where to invest, how to invest, and how to improve and expand their business. And we have few exceptions to the rule that, once privatized, labor practices improve. As a result of improved productivity, wages and earnings actually rise. Enormous amounts of new business come to the company as a result of its new spirit of enterprise and participation, knocking on the head the idea that, once in the private sector, assets are somehow spirited away and are no longer there for the greater good of the economy they help support.

An important part of the process, then, has been the economic re-education of the country. By the mid-1970s, many people had forgotten that price is a good device to match supply and demand. They had forgotten that a subsidy in one place is likely to destroy jobs elsewhere as a result of the tax or borrowing effects on the economy of supporting the subsidized job. And they had forgotten that pouring money into a bankrupt state enterprise, if it is making the wrong things or has forgotten about its customers, will only delay the inevitable day of reckoning. These things became visible as public sector fiefdoms were opened to competitive enterprise. Take, for example, the unromantic but important case of the Intercity Coach Service, which plies the motorways of our country. It was once regulated and heavily licensed.

When deregulation took place and new entrants were allowed, opponents said it would be the end of intercity coach services, that there would be no way the market could sustain the system. But the Minister of Transport went ahead, and the results were stunning. Fares fell drastically, and the number of people using the coaches shot upward. The industry turned into an exciting, high-growth operation in which passenger volumes rose 70 percent on the main intercity connections. Suddenly there were coaches with telephones and videos and toilets, and all kinds of add-on excitement to make a coach journey something to remember. This makes politics exciting because, while a citizen may have no interest in public borrowing or in the accounting practices of state enterprises, he is interested in whether his phone works. He is interested in how he can get from A to B. He is interested in the price, quality, and variety of products and services.

Our final theme is that an end can be made to some of the enormous losses of state enterprise. Again, it has been said that this is inconceivable, that it can be done only at the expense of enormous redundancies, closure of service, or failure to supply essential goods and services. An analysis I have done of the steel industry, where the bulk is still in public ownership, shows that job losses as a percentage of initial employment had been far greater during the decade of heavy subsidy than they had been in the private sector, where there was not only little subsidy but also heavy competition from subsidized nationalized industry. The same was borne out in the automobile industry. British Leyland received £2.5 billion in subsidies and lost many more jobs than unsubsidized, competing car makers in the private sector. To clinch the argument, after the privatization of Jaguar—a part of British Leyland that many thought needed to be closed down at the time—the company added employees and is now much bigger than it was before. Competition is the best way to ensure customer interest. But we have also found it necessary to generate some regulation. In the privatization of British Telecom and British Gas we have set forth rules that give the customer more protection than he had before.

In conclusion, privatization has grown in the United Kingdom partly because interest has been built in its favor and partly because the government has had the political will to create the necessary committees and undertake the methods of disposal that lead to a vigorous and successful privatization program. In the Treasury, there is a minister charged with the privatization program. The Prime Minister supports the policy. Now Cabinet ministers see that privatization not only refreshes parts of the public sector, but enlivens their popularity.

We live in a debt-ridden world. One of our biggest problems is countries bowed down with debt who do not know how to raise the money they need and who are worried about the political consequences of too much belt-tightening or too much taxation. In such circumstances, the only thing that can keep the wheels of the world economy turning is to increase the amount of equity in order to stop the growth of debt. For an individual nation, that means selling equity to savers and investors, whether they be domestic or foreign.

We have developed a simple device for preventing undesirable takeovers, including foreign takeovers. Even where 100 percent of the ordinary dividend-bearing equity in a company is sold, the government retains a single "golden share." This share has only one power: the emergency power to vote on a change of ownership of the shareholdings as a whole. As a result, there have been no takeover bids. This could block an unwelcome domestic monopoly takeover just as it could a foreign takeover. Finally, investment from overseas in the equity of privatizing companies can be part of a country's strategy to offset a trade imbalance.

20

Ted M. Ohashi

Privatization: The Case of British Columbia

Back in the early 1970s, when ideas about privatization were first introduced in British Columbia, there was a saying: people who are experts in privatization are like men who know a hundred different ways to make love to a woman but don't know any women. There was some degree of truth to the analogy in those days, but things have certainly changed since then. Privatization has grown to the point where it now touches many of our lives.

British Columbia is the westernmost province of Canada, a developed country with a relatively sophisticated capital market, of which our province represents about 10 percent. In the early 1970s, *Barron's Magazine* called the province the 'Chile of the North' in reference to the socialist Allende regime. Ideas changed with the election of a new premier of British Columbia, and privatization had his full support. In fact it was his idea, and he assembled a group of investment firms,

including my own, to plan the program. Having a committee comprised
only of investment bankers was a mistake: it did not have the input
of politicians or the commercial banking system, which led to unneces-
sary problems later on. When such committees are structured, it is a
good idea to involve important sectors of the economy and the political scene so that their support is enlisted in advance. It is especially
critical to have full political support, because changes will undoubt-
edly have to be made, concessions will have to be given, and political
hurdles will have to be overcome. These can be accomplished only with
the full support of the people who are able to make those decisions.

Our privatization committee took an inventory of the two dozen
assets that were available to us to privatize. Some of them were generating earnings; some were not. We selected five assets from the
inventory—three in forest products, one in oil and gas, and one in gas
transmission. We created a new holding company, transferred the assets
into it, and called it the British Columbia Resource Investment Corporation (BCRIC). In return for those assets the government received
a certain number of common shares in the company.

In forming the new company, we selected a board of directors
restricted to business people: five very qualified, high-profile people
whose responsibilities did not conflict with any of our assets. It was
a small group: once those affiliated with forestry, oil, gas, and gas delivery were eliminated, due to a potential conflict of interest, the list was
quickly narrowed. There were no representatives of government anywhere in the management of the company. We hired independent businessmen as directors; they in turn hired business people as managers;
then the company was privatized.

Decision on Shares

As investment people, we went through a long period of considering
complicated forms of securities, suggesting that some common shares
be sold to investors and some restricted dividend shares be given to
the government. At one point we considered petroleum notes, and
preferreds, and convertible preferreds. But all these considerations overlooked the fact that our government was simply trying to accomplish

a reversal of the socialist practices of the government it had replaced. It didn't care whether it got money for the assets or not, it just wanted to get rid of them and return them to the private sector. If we had recognized that earlier, we would have saved ourselves a lot of time and effort in internal planning.

The privatization was done by giving the shares the government owned to the residents of British Columbia. The reason we gave shares only to residents of the province is that the assets were owned by the provincial government; that is, the government that represents those people. We divided the number of shares the government owned, 15 million, by the number of people we estimated were living in the province, which worked out to very close to five shares each. It is interesting to note that there was an increase in the number of residents in the province applying for Canadian citizenship in order to qualify for what amounted to $30 Canadian worth of shares. At the same time that we did the actual privatization we also undertook an underwriting of the shares that were sold to investors, again strictly within British Columbia. Since these were shares from the company's treasury, the money that was raised went back into the company.

The free distribution and underwriting of shares took place during a three-month period. After that period closed, there was a six-week period in which there was no trading. Then the shares were listed, and everyone was free to do with their shares as they saw fit. But there was informal trading of shares during the six weeks prior to official listing: people were out in the streets offering to buy them, or merchants were offering to accept them in return for merchandise.

During the planning process we felt that something like two-thirds to three-quarters of the free shares would be taken up. In fact, 86 percent of the shares that were available were distributed. The 14 percent that were left over were then immediately owned by the government following the privatization. The government gave those shares to a foundation in British Columbia, and there was a holding period associated with the gift. The foundation has subsequently liquidated its holdings, so that the shares were, in fact, totally given away.

The coincident share underwriting raised $487.5 million, more than twice as much as the previous Canadian common stock issue record and surpassed only by two others in the United States. The company started with this capital and made one significant and several less significant acquisitions. Some of the funds were allocated toward exploration on the oil and gas properties, and some were used to make relatively minor purchases of other companies that complemented the portfolio. Again, we did not set out to underwrite nearly $500 million. Everyone in the province received five free shares, and each of those people was offered another 5,000 at $6 a share. Altogether, people subscribed for $485 million worth. Today the shares are worth $2 each, the low end of a range that has reached a high of $9 between 1978 and today. The difference reflects the lower valuation of the resource assets.

A number of factors explain why people invested in BCRIC. There was a positive pricing outlook for the forest products, oil, and gas industries, which were doing well and expected to continue to do so, which they did for awhile. The period in question, 1978-79, was a period of high inflation. There also was the perception that such a government-sponsored transaction wouldn't be allowed to go bad, and that it therefore must be good. There was no such guarantee, but people couldn't be convinced of this. Finally, the premier of the province took an active part in campaigning for the new company, claiming it was something that all the citizens in the province should support.

Risks Avoided

Twice in the two-and-a-half-year period from the time the committee was created to the time the issue was completed, the whole plan nearly collapsed. The first point was during the planning process, before we regained sight of the most important thing our government wanted to accomplish. As mentioned earlier, some very complicated, convoluted packages of securities were put together as supposed payment for the assets, packages so complicated that they became acceptable to nobody, even to those who dreamed them up. The planning nearly collapsed before we finally saw the simplest answer to the whole payment question: give the shares away.

The second problem was political. The premier of our province chose the three-month period in which distribution was taking place to call an election. To those of us in planning, it was horrifying to think that in the middle of the distribution period the government that acquired the assets in the first place might come back to power. The premier's political instincts turned out to be right: he won by a very large majority.

Results

The company exists today, operating in the same areas, though it has changed quite a lot from the company we privatized. Its shares trade on the stock exchange and it is fully competitive, owned entirely by nongovernment investors. But the basic difference is that decisions are now made in the competitive environment of the private sector as opposed to the public sector.

The shareholding is very different today from the initial shareholding because initially the giveaway and underwriting of shares was to individuals within the province. Shareholding has subsequently spread across the country and switched to the so-called institutional investors: the pension funds, mutual funds, and banks.

There are three points regarding the BCRIC experience that are especially relevant to LDC (less-developed country) privatization programs. The first regards public education. In this case there was much spontaneous education taking place, because those who had never before owned a financial asset suddenly owned one. The educational process was something to behold, even in our supposedly developed country. It was a natural subject for newspaper, radio, and television treatment, as well as bank and investment firm advertising: this is what your shares are, this is what they mean, this is how you can buy or sell them.

The plan itself was not without its critics when it was first announced, some of whom presented analyses that were just plain wrong and revealed a total misunderstanding of how corporations run, how they are put together, and what it means to be a shareholder. But there was a lot of dialogue going on in the media as well as among families over the back fence. There was a material benefit simply in terms of education about corporations and how they work.

The second point is that assessment of the LDC assets that will be privatized first is crucial. There is a division of opinion on this; I believe the first few privatizations should be given the greatest chance of success, and that they should contain the most commercially viable assets available. This is not to say that an LDC government has to ignore assets that are less attractive. But to get a long-term privatization program started off on the right foot, begin it with a viable asset. Later, less viable assets can be included — by bundling assets in a holding company, for instance.

Finally, LDCs should expect a great deal of informal trading. People will generate interest and momentum in learning about stock ownership. Even in areas of low literacy, people will talk among themselves and educate one another, and a little government publicity will go far.

Privatization:
The Case of Turkey

There is much to be learned from the experiences of various countries in the design and implementation of privatization policies, however different the characteristics of the country or the nature of and reasoning behind privatization policies may be. There is skepticism about privatization reports. In less-developed countries (LDCs), the problems of state economic enterprises are recognized, but many countries feel nothing can be done to solve these problems. I believe that if certain policies are required in order to restructure economies and make them more effective, hard decisions will have to be made. I shall concentrate in this paper on the legal framework, design, and implementation of privatization programs; practical difficulties; and prospects for the future. Before embarking on this, I shall give a brief description of the change in the course of Turkish economic policy since 1980 and the place of state economic enterprises (SEEs) in the Turkish economy. The country's privatization policy can best be understood in this context.

Since 1980, our economic management has been radically transformed. Turkey has moved away from an inward-looking attitude of heavy state intervention toward allowing greater play of market forces and increased liberalization of the economy. There is a greater understanding and appreciation of the idea that the economy cannot be managed through restrictions, protections, penalties, and bureaucratic controls. Many policies and regulatory changes have been implemented.

Government intervention in the economy has been reduced to the minimum level required. Price controls have been removed. Export activities have been encouraged. A realistic rate of exchange has been established through continuous adjustments. A realistic rate of interest has been established. Foreign trade and payments have been liberalized. The economy has been opened up to international competition. State subsidies to SEEs have been phased out. State investments have been limited to infrastructure and energy projects.

Private investors have been allowed to enter sectors that had always been thought of as the exclusive domain of the state. The banking sector has been deregulated. In order to activate capital markets in an orderly manner, a capital market law has been enacted. To attract more foreign investment, a secure economic environment has been created, and foreigners have been given the right to transfer dividend earnings, proceeds of sale, and liquidation of assets that they own. Investment incentives are applied to all concerned, without differentiating between domestic and foreign investors. Funds have been established outside the slow budgetary process to finance infrastructure, housing, and industry-related defense projects.

It did not take long to achieve positive results with the program. Inflation has been controlled and reduced, although its present level is not yet satisfactory. Exports have been increased more than threefold, from just over $2 billion in 1980 to $8 billion in 1985. The share of industrial goods in the composition of exports has risen from 35 percent to almost 80 percent in five years. The balance of payments has improved enough to improve credibility substantially in international financial markets. The budget deficit has been reduced significantly. Structural changes in the economy have been realized, and sound financing policies have been used.

State Economic Enterprises

Turkey's privatization program must be evaluated in light of developments and changes that have been taking place in the Turkish economy, and must be seen as an attempt to improve the economy by widening the scope of involvement of the private sector and narrowing that of the state. SEEs were the result of conscious industrialization policies during the 1930s. Initially the main reasons for the development of SEEs were the insufficiency of entrepreneurial skills and capital accumulation in the private sector and the belief that SEEs were the engines of industrial and regional development. The enterprises were to work as effectively and productively as other business enterprises. The founders of SEEs even considered privatizing and establishing SEE clauses charging the Cabinet with exploring opportunities for selling shares of SEEs to the public. Proceeds of these sales were to be used to finance new industrial projects.

SEEs did achieve certain objectives, though their successes generated dogmatism: the belief that the state sector does certain things better became the belief SEEs do everything better. The privatization clauses in SEE laws were never put into force, and the government's scope of activity in the economy increased continuously. Now SEEs employ more than 600,000 people and account for 30 percent of total investment and 15 percent of gross domestic product. This sector, which claims much of the economy's resources, has been able to deliver little in terms of efficiency, productivity, and quality of goods and services produced.

In the 1980s, the government has taken drastic measures to improve the efficiency of SEEs. All the exemptions and advantages they enjoyed were abolished, and managers have been allowed to determine the prices of their products. Still, the propensity for showing losses and the poor service of much of the public sector seem incurable. Since these enterprises cannot go bankrupt, there is no compulsion to compete or excel. Financial targets can ultimately be ignored. Even if SEEs are deregulated there is no final sanction on the state enterprise. Government regulation of SEEs is more difficult than the regulation of private enterprises.

Taking all of this into consideration, the government of Turkey has taken steps to liberalize and privatize SEEs. With the passage in February 1984 of the Law Concerning the Encouragement of Savings and Acceleration of Public Investments, the legal framework for privatization and liberalization of SEEs was prepared. The aims of this law are to promote savings by providing stable and reliable income, accelerate investments with the aid of a swift financing mechanism, and render SEEs efficient by opening them to private capital participation.

The law introduces four major instruments for the realization of these objectives: revenue-sharing bonds, equity shares, transfer of SEE operating rights, and the Public Participation Fund. Revenue-sharing bonds are documents allowing legal and real persons' participation in the revenues accruing from infrastructural facilities owned by public institutions and establishments. Bridges, dams, power stations, expressways, railways, telecommunications systems, ports, and airports are included in the definition of infrastructural projects. By letting real and legal persons have a share in the revenues of these facilities for specified periods while the state maintains ownership, a new pool of savings has been created. The result can be viewed as partial privatization.

Equity shares and transfer of operating rights are instruments directly related to SEEs. All the proceeds from these instruments will accrue to the Public Participation Fund, set up outside the budget. Revenues from the operation of facilities for which revenue-sharing bonds have been issued are also pooled in the fund, which is used to finance infrastructural facilities for which revenue-sharing bonds will be issued in the future, SEEs that may be privatized if necessary, and investments in regions with development priority. The law mentions the flotation of SEE shares as a means to privatize these enterprises and obtain the nation's participation in the national wealth. By withdrawing from industrial and commercial activities and by trying to improve the industrial infrastructure, and hence by creating a suitable environment for the private sector, the government will support industrial development through attractive incentives.

Planning

In the design and implementation of the privatization program, the Administration has been organizing its activities around the following assumptions:

- The creation of huge, crowded, and unmanageable state machinery is not desirable;
- Cooperation and active participation of all governmental agencies is essential; and
- Outside help on a contractual basis is desirable.

Within the Administration, a core group has been established whose duty is to prepare SEEs for privatization. A parallel group has been established in the State Planning Organization, as has a group headed by the State Minister to evaluate all works with a view to privatization and to take matters to the Housing Development and Public Participation Board for decision. Currently, the planning of privatization and disengagement of SEEs from the state are taking place. These studies include:

- analysis of sectors in which SEEs are operating;
- determination of the status and place of an SEE or SEE business unit in a particular sector;
- financial and operational analyses of SEEs and SEE business units;
- preparation of policies aimed at solving personnel problems, and the treatment of accumulated indemnity and severance payments to SEE personnel employed under work law;
- analysis of regional conditions where SEEs or SEE business units are located, including population, economic development, business activity, and business linkage between the SEE and the region;
- determination of the ideal capital structure for SEEs;
- determination of funding mechanisms whereby SEE debts, especially foreign debts, can be taken care of;
- analyses of capital and money markets in Turkey;
- valuation of SEEs and SEE business units and pricing of their shares;
- design of privatization programs;
- design of mechanisms whereby SEE personnel will become shareholders in companies in which they work;

- determination of marketing policies and strategies for SEE corporate stocks;
- determination of conditions whereby SEEs' operating rights will be transferred to the private sector; and
- turning SEEs or SEE business units into limited liability corporations governed by the Turkish Commercial Code.

Sectoral rehabilitation projects have been commissioned by the State Planning Organization with an emphasis on determining the privatization potential of SEEs operating in those sectors. Similar studies in other sectors will soon follow. Another study commissioned by the State Planning Organization is the Privatization Master Plan Study, which will examine privatization objectives, capital markets, key privatization factors, investor preferences, economic and financial viability of SEEs, and legal and accounting problems. It will classify SEEs according to their privatization potential and prepare plans and timetables for all the SEEs, as well as specific plans for those with the highest privatization potential. Initial signs are that the potential of SEEs to become viable enterprises is great, offering all investors, whether domestic, foreign, corporate, or individual, a chance to direct their savings and funds to new, productive investments.

Implementation

The first privatization decision taken by the High Economic Council was the privatization of Turkish Airlines, the national carrier. Preparations have been made to determine the best method of privatization, and to prepare the company for it. Sale of shares to the employees of the company and to the public will be followed by sale to domestic private companies and foreign investors.

Several industrial projects started by SEEs in the 1970s were stopped in the 1980s for several reasons, most important of which was the shortage of financing. Land had been purchased for these projects, and buildings and other facilities had been constructed. The High Council decided to sell the incomplete investments to private investors, and authorized the Administration to implement the decision. The

Administration has offered these investments with the condition that they be used for industrial purposes. The response from the private sector has been good, and it is hoped that three of the investments will be turned over to the private sector soon.

The High Council also decided to sell shares of certain SEEs and subsidiaries and the Administration began working on these cases. Preparations to transfer the operating rights of other SEE business units to private corporations have begun, and one dairy factory has been leased. Leasing of SEE business units will continue, with the aim of achieving efficiency in operating these plants.

All these examples illustrate that the structural issues of privatization are being addressed from all angles, and that the government is committed to privatization as a component of its industrial development strategy. Through it, the state's role in economic and financial activities will be minimized, government subsidies will be abolished completely, and competition will be introduced to produce goods and services at lower costs.

In the implementation of the privatization program, the main intent of the government is to increase efficiency and productivity, to promote the development of capital markets, and to widen share ownership, thus meeting social goals in a better way. State ownership does not guarantee that the social and economic interests of the people are served well, and the history of these establishments shows that they have not been doing much social service other than consuming rare resources. Now there are entrepreneurs in the country who can buy and run these establishments, and private savings and wealth are at such levels that they can be used for the transfer of state assets to the private sector.

Difficulties

Since this is the case, what are the practical difficulties in the implementation of this policy? The most important appears to be the present state of capital markets in Turkey and the distrust of small shareholders due to losses they have encountered. A similar difficulty has plagued banks and intermediary institutions. Consequently, savings have been used for unproductive investments such as gold and real estate, and their investment choices have been very limited. Before 1980, gold and real estate represented the main instruments for people's savings during periods of extremely low relative interest rates. But since 1980, a major portion of savings has shifted to the banking system as interest rates were increased.

As part of an attempt to regulate and activate capital markets, a capital market law was in enacted in 1981. Under this law, a Capital Market Board has been established to undertake the duties of developing capital markets in Turkey. The law essentially regulates primary market activities and declares the principle of security issues and necessary qualities and duties of intermediaries. The Capital Market Board has the authority to permit public offerings of all kinds of securities issues except those of the public sector. Granting such permission, the CMB has to consider the sufficiency and truthfulness of the information supplied by the company and take the public interest into consideration.

Banks and stock exchange brokers have been authorized to act as intermediaries in the primary issues market. The formation of investment companies and mutual funds to operate in this market has also been allowed. To activate secondary markets, regulations have been introduced stating the principles of listing and trading procedures, and the Istanbul Stock Exchange has been reactivated. In Turkey, joint stock companies are mainly in the form of family holdings, and as they are more prone to debt financing than equity financing, few companies have opened or will open their capital to the public. Through these regulatory changes, capital markets should reactivate, and public flotation of SEE shares will supply the capital market with securities that are essential for its development. Different types of securities have been developed to meet different investor demands, but still more needs to be done in this field, especially given the effects of inflation. Savers' expectations concerning dividends and capital appreciation must be met, and people must be encouraged to keep their wealth in the form of financial securities rather than gold or real estate. The ways in which these problems are tackled will be crucial to the success of the privatization program.

By 1986, 200 billion Turkish lira worth of revenue-sharing bonds had been issued, and the last issue, worth 60 billion, was sold in a matter of hours. This shows that if public expectations are met, demand will pose no great problem. With the public flotation of SEE shares and new issues of revenue-sharing bonds, supply-side questions concerning the development of capital markets will be partially answered, and this, in fact, will direct private joint stock companies to opt for public flotation of their shares.

Finally we come to the question of prospects for the future. We believe that if the privatization policy is designed and implemented properly, and the timing and volume of issues are right, the policy will achieve its aims of improving industrial efficiency and activating capital markets.

22

Donald Shay

Privatization:
The Case of Grenada

Grenada presents a good case for discussion of planning privatization because the privatization of its economy is recent—November 1986—and because as a small country that has undertaken a comprehensive approach to the privatization of all state enterprises, it may serve as an example for other countries undergoing the process.

The state portfolio contained twenty-nine enterprises with an annual revenue of ED$50 million, or about US$20 million. The enterprises included an ice cream dairy, a publishing house, utilities, telecommunications and electrical companies, and financial institutions. Also included were civil works companies, public services, and hotels. Structurally, some of these companies operated as government departments within a ministry. Others operated as statutory bodies outside of specific ministry responsibility, but with a board of directors, often represented by a ministry. Still others operated as share companies with a board appointed by the government.

Of the twenty-nine enterprises, three were profitable. Collectively they usually broke even. Two were banks so profitable that they alone compensated for deficits run by most of the others. The majority of the companies operated at 10 to 30 percent capacity. With improved marketing and work incentives, one of these companies might have tripled capacity and sales. The phone and electrical companies, however, were starved for capital with far more demand than they could meet; the former had a waiting list of 2,000 names. They were highly leveraged, with terrible debt-for-equity ratios and little chance of an infusion of funds from outside.

The Steps

We began by establishing a working group, an objective body to evaluate information and make recommendations to the government on what to do with the portfolio. In order to make sure that we had a broad spectrum of representation, we chose members from various sectors of the community: a banker, an accountant, a nominee from the trade union council, one from the chamber of commerce, a representative from the ministry of finance, and the chairman of the local development bank.

The second step was to gather and analyze data on each enterprise — marketing, finance, operations, quality of management — to try to understand the business and the commercial viability of each enterprise. We began by simply reviewing financial statements, most of which were out of date. Few of the companies had been audited, but all had income statements and some also had balance sheets. Next we visited each company for one to three days to meet with the managing directors, senior functional managers, various ministry officials, and sometimes customers. We also talked with competitors and suppliers to learn about company markets. Late in the series of visits, we discussed with ministers and managers their views of privatization strategies. This was a critical step, and would have been even more beneficial if it had been done earlier in the process.

Loaded with business and marketing facts, we analyzed each company for operating efficiency, capacity, market, and overall commercial viability. The critical question was each company's potential to survive in the open market. To our surprise, the answer in most cases was affirmative; there was a market for the product or service provided by each business. We then met with government ministers to review the study process and hear their views on the enterprises. And this is key: we were dealing with a coalition government, so we needed to understand how each of the ministers felt about privatization and where each one stood on those specific enterprises for which he had responsibility.

Following that, the working group reviewed each enterprise based on the information developed in the inventory, considered privatization options, and made recommendations of options for each enterprise to the Prime Minister. He reviewed our options and presented them to his Cabinet in a formal Cabinet paper.

The Decisions

Through a series of discussions in November 1986, the Cabinet made final decisions and moved to implement them immediately. The decisions on the twenty-nine enterprises were as follows:

- full and immediate divestment for seven companies;
- gradually sold shares of two banks with intent to divest completely within three years;
- slated two companies for sale in future, when project money would have to be regenerated;
- planned for sale of two companies receiving donor assistance after funding is cut off;
- sold minority interest of one company and contracted for private management;
- planned for management contracting out of three companies;
- planned for conversion of three companies to statutory bodies;
- restructured one company and demonopolized import function;
- sold liquidated assets of two companies;
- merged three companies and retained them as statutory bodies;

- deferred decisions on three companies pending more information.

Conclusion

The rapid implementation of Grenada's privatization program is unusual; most enterprises are nationalized over decades and therefore require time to be privatized. Our greatest asset was political commitment; privatization is above all a political process. Working teams need to understand the politics and engage ministeries early on. Stemming from this most critical point are a few other observations.

First, political decision-makers are most comfortable when given the opportunity to choose from among a variety of options. The Prime Minister of Grenada had difficulty with the process when its focus was purely divestment, as opposed to less radical privatization measures that gave him more choice. It became clear in our discussions that having a range of carefully thought out options was crucial to gaining his support. Second, it should come as no surprise that governments are most sensitive to the impact of privatization on employment and on the national treasury. Discussions will often focus on these issues and may be very delicate. Third, the greatest costs of state enterprises are often hidden and thus overlooked. Operating subsidies are obvious, but these are often the least of the real costs, which include human and other resource inefficiencies. For example, Grenada's poor utility services were a drain on the economy far beyond their operating subsidies; as with many of the twenty-nine companies in our privatization program, they were operating at a fraction of their capacity. Underutilization of existing infrastructure and assets represents an expensive opportunity cost. A fourth point is that, while underutilization has many sources, the most observable in Grenada was lack of worker incentive. The manager of Grenada's state-owned dairies earned the same salary whether he sold a hundred ice cream bars or twenty times that. Incentives will spur operations toward capacity.

The final point is that a common understanding of each enterprise to be privatized is crucial to effective change. We found that members of the government, the private sector, and donor communities all had different or uninformed views on the enterprises. After our working group presented a consistent set of facts, however, consensus usually could be reached on privatization options for each enterprise. Building a constituency in support of the program extends beyond the elite group of decision-makers: the press and the media ought to be engaged to educate the public. There will be a host of opposing forces for any privatization program, and it is the working group's responsibility to help the public understand how the program will be of benefit.

Part VI

Conclusion

23

Steve H. Hanke

Toward a People's Capitalism

Perhaps the most interesting thing about privatization is its popularity. Four or five years ago the word "privatization" could not be found in economic and political vocabularies. Now the word can be found in popular dictionaries, and talk is everywhere about it; even if one discounts what are often the excessive enthusiasms connected to fashions of the moment—for economics and politics are no different than other domains—the outpouring of news about privatization everywhere in the world must be considered astonishing.

It is probably true that the privatization enthusiasm varies from place to place. In Africa, for instance, James Brooke writes in a recent *New York Times* article that interest in privatization is motivated by the desire to correct past failures of development policy and cut the red ink of chronic, money-losing state enterprises.[1] He writes:

> Twenty-five years ago, many newly independent African countries turned to the state to lead economic growth. Unfortunately, in most cases, growth did not come. Of Africa's 52 countries, 29 were poorer in 1986 than in 1960, according to World Bank figures on per-capita gross national product.

Mr. Brooke captures the spirit of the change in describing a Frenchman, working near Red Star Square in Cotonou, Benin. "Everything
was nationalized," he quotes the Frenchman as saying, "and everything
was failing. . . . Now they are trying to privatize everything."

In considering the matter ideologically, one would expect the conservative governments of Margaret Thatcher in Great Britain and
Jacques Chirac in France to favor privatization. But this economic revolution is not limited to conservative governments. Mr. Brooke is writing about the plans of *Marxist* governments — in Angola, Benin, and
the Congo — to sell money-losing state companies.

That there has been a shift of thinking about "what works" is
undeniable. Such an ideological shift would in fact be hard to believe
if similar shifts were not also evident in the largest of the Marxist-
Leninist countries — China and the Soviet Union.

Beyond the intellectual and practical attraction of private ownership and market mechanisms, there is a political factor that I think
accounts for privatization's extraordinary popularity. While the traditional analysis of the political forces that generate increasing government spending contends that the *concentrated* interests of the few who
receive the government's largess outweigh the *diffused* interests of the
taxpayers, privatization, properly designed, has turned this on its head,
at least in Western democracies: it has pitted a political constituency
with a concentrated interest (the people who will own shares in the
privatized company) against one (the general public) with only a weak,
diffused interest in maintaining public ownership. In this case, the weak-
ness of the diffused, general interest for maintaining public ownership
will be particularly evident if the state-owned company is losing money.
Managers and employees of public firms, as well as those who receive
subsidized or unsubsidized output from public enterprises do represent a concentrated, special interest; they might oppose privatization.
Allow me simply to mention here that these two groups of public enterprise beneficiaries can be neutralized, if not won over, simply by insuring
that they are allowed to participate in the benefits of privatization,
through either higher wages, ownership rights, lower output prices,
or higher quality services.

The British experience exemplifies how privatization can be used
to generate political as well as economic benefits. Mrs. Thatcher has

learned that the actual sale of assets and shares presents an enormous (and one would think obvious) opportunity to build a constituency of political support, especially for future privatization. Prior to Mrs. Thatcher's government, denationalizations were typically implemented by the "private placement" of shares to companies or small groups of individuals. In many cases, the new owners were merely the old owners who originally had their shares nationalized.

In consequence, privatizations did little to broaden capital ownership within the general public. In addition, privatizations failed to take note of Joseph Schumpeter's observation that all property rights are not equal in their ability to generate loyalties and political support.[2] Ownership in "abstract forms," such as shares of stock held by the general public, generates far less loyalty than ownership of one's own home, business, or place of employment. Consequently, in England there were few who were devoted defenders of private ownership and who opposed labor government renationalization of private enterprises. Britain has experienced a cycle of nationalization-denationalization; Mrs. Thatcher's privatization strategy is designed to terminate this cycle by broadening ownership and by making it more than an "abstract form."

Britain's new privatization strategy is built on a very different political analysis. Under privatization, firms are now sold in public offerings to a broad constituency of *individual* shareholders. This broad constituency includes potential detractors of privatization, i.e., current managers and employees of nationalized firms and users of the output of the nationalized enterprises. Hence, these shareholders become personally interested and involved in the sale and thus become the basis of a powerful political constituency supporting future privatization and opposing renationalization.

To illustrate the power of this approach, in one sale *ninety-six percent* of the members of a particular labor union bought shares in a newly privatized firm, ignoring the union's campaign to persuade them to do otherwise. All of those who purchased shares have realized huge profits, and all have (not surprisingly) become great supporters of privatization.

The logical consequence of this is that today between seventy-five and eighty percent of the British public consistently support privatization regardless of their political attitudes on other issues or their feelings toward the Thatcher government. A similar thing has happened in France in response to the privatization program of Prime Minister Jacques Chirac. In the face of this support, the British Labor Party and the French Socialist Party have conspicuously de-emphasized its longstanding commitment to renationalization. A great deal of this change is the result of seeing privatization as more a political than economic action and structuring privatization strategies to build political constituencies.

Managing Successful Privatization

Initiating a successful privatization program requires developing a strategy with certain essential parts.

1. Before one even thinks about developing a plan for privatization, one must create an economic environment hospitable to private ownership. This issue must precede everything, for if it is not settled, no privatization plan can go anywhere. As Peter Thomas, Larry White, and I note in respective chapters, this task involves reviewing the tax system and law regarding property rights to be sure that the tax climate is sympathetic and that a basis exists in law for private property rights that ensure and protect value for new owners and stimulate the development of local capital markets. This issue — a great deal can obviously be said about it — goes to the entire legal structure in a country, whether it encourages or discourages private ownership. There is no space here to state the principle more than generally: the general economic climate must be conducive to private ownership before one can even think about trying to develop a successful program for privatization.

2. Begin with a serious program of public information. Once one has reviewed the tax and legal systems and is satisfied they contain no serious problems, the first step in thinking about how to privatize is to build a political constituency for privatization, a sympathetic environment in which further privatization will be possible and encouraged. This is discussed by Lance Marston and others. Selling privatization to both the public and private sectors is more complicated than simply establishing a sympathetic environment, though that is certainly important. Public education must be an education based more on action than words, especially in the beginning. This means taking on the least controversial objects for it, doing it slowly, and doing it successfully—all of these things are important for "public education." It means, in short, developing priorities that allow the public to perceive the benefits of privatization, and show it can be accomplished without great difficulty (See #4 below).

3. Organize a training program and develop specialists in the technical dimensions of the issue. To ensure that initial privatization ventures are perceived as successful both by the policy audiences and by the general public, it is crucial that, before one begins selecting targets, one develops a stable of well-trained specialists to manage the technical side of the plan. This means having people well versed in all of the enormously varied techniques for doing privatization—from contracting out public services to divesting ownership in publicly-owned companies, either by sale of stock or even (at one extreme) simply giving the company away.

4. Especially at the outset, pick targets for privatization that minimize difficulties and guarantee success. This task involves establishing priorities and is extremely important. Everything can't be privatized at once, and trying to do so only means that nothing will be privatized. Instead, selected targets that can be privatized with relative ease must be identified. This is especially important in Third World countries and in countries that have little experience with privatization.

Focusing on success—especially on the need for *perceptions* of success—tends to lead in an interesting and counter-intuitive direction. Focusing on success means *avoiding*, especially at the outset, companies that are sustaining the largest losses—causing the largest drains on the public purse. While privatization of such companies would bring the greatest efficiency gains, bringing greatest benefit to the public treasury, one must avoid the temptation to focus too much on economics, while forgetting politics. Such companies are difficult to privatize precisely because their losses make them difficult to market. For this reason, it is best—again, especially at the outset—to concentrate on privatizing firms that do not suffer terrible financial difficulties, firms that can be prepared with relative ease for public sale.

The central point in this task is to focus on *perceptions*. It is not enough for the first privatization to be (actually) successful if it is perceived to fail. The perception is crucial because it will determine the public response. If it is perceived to be difficult, not to be successful, that will probably kill all interest in it—perhaps for as long as a generation, until another generation can be interested again.

5. Select techniques and strategies that will maximize the supporting political constituency. Once targets are selected, this task is crucial, and here the Thatcher government has set the standard. The key is finding a constituency that will support privatization, and neutralizing or co-opting special interests who might oppose it. As Lance Marston notes, this suggests that an important part of preparing for privatization involves making sure that a lot of people will benefit, and that a portion of the beneficiaries be potential opponents who have been won over, or to put it bluntly, *bought off*. It is just as important that the beneficiaries *know* it well ahead of time.

6. Prepare the company for privatization, if necessary by investing in it. As Madsen Pirie and Peter Young note, sometimes effort and even perhaps money must be invested to make companies attractive to the private market. It is important because many companies will not attract private investors at what the public perceives as a fair price without special investments being made to upgrade the enterprises.

This is perhaps *the* central element in successful privatization. Preparing for privatization involves a series of things, including public education, but especially things that improve the prospects for profitability of the company or entity being privatized. Establishing the prospect for profits is the critical step in making the entity marketable— attractive in a market.

Establishing marketability involves both political and economic costs. They include overcoming concentrated opposition from interest groups who either stand to lose from privatization or who simply feel *uncertain* about its outcome. There is an old saying that people tend to prefer a known evil to an unknown good. It is not necessary that someone will actually lose from privatization for him to oppose it; it is enough that he is *uncertain* about the outcome to ensure his opposition.

Typically, the target for privatization is a public company that has existed over a long period on public subsidies. If privatized, the assumption will be that it must survive without such subsidies. Pirie reports that in England many nationalized enterprises are undercapitalized and have an excessive work force. Preparing them for privatization will mean, therefore (among other things), making investments, paring back the workforce, and building up the capital stock so that the company is appealing to private investors.

7. Avoid the temptation to suspend the special privileges often found in public enterprises. In publicly-owned firms, like government bureaucracies, the employees — both the managers and workforce — often enjoy enormous and unusual privileges. Pirie and Young strongly advise that no matter how outrageous these privileges may seem, it is essential that in preparing for privatization that a commitment be made not to suspend these privileges. For if the threat of suspension is heard, the immediate result will be enormous, concentrated opposition and probably an end to any serious possibility of privatizing that particular firm.

In dealing with special privileges, the best approach may be to *buy them out* with a cash settlement — for instance, to buy out a pension plan — because in the long run a buy-out will be an efficient way of dealing with an important element of the transaction costs.

Some Cautions

As noted above, the worldwide interest in privatization is extraordinary. It is particularly so when one considers that privatization involves a monopoly (the government) voluntarily yielding control to private parties (those who end up controlling the privatized entity). However, the concentration of the private interest in this case is turning out to be stronger than the concentration of interests in governments themselves — hence this extraordinary transfer.

I have discussed a number of reasons for the new privatization enthusiasm. It may be easiest to summarize its *political* appeal by noting that privatization can be a genuine "people's capitalism," and the very notion of that communicates why it has generated the momentum it has.

Despite the economic, social, and political values associated with privatization, it is important to note some cautions. The need for caution is especially important because one moment's exaggerated enthusiasm is often the next moment's defeated expectation. This would be a great pity in the case of privatization, which can achieve important and constructive things in developed and developing countries alike.

The major caution is directed at the hope that privatization will automatically improve economic efficiency and cut costs. Where privatization de-monopolizes a public function—when it sells a business in a competitive industry, for instance—the movement from public monopoly to private competition will certainly change the incentive structure, and efficiencies and savings should result. James Brooke cites a number of examples of this from Africa in the article mentioned earlier. But where privatization simply transfers a government monopoly to a private one—especially where privatization takes the form of contracting out public services to a sole-source private company—then it does not change those incentives. In such instances, rather than reducing costs, privatization may end up actually *increasing* costs (especially when one adds costs of surveillance and monitoring that would go with contracting out).

In sounding this caution, I should note that Madsen Pirie, who has had a great deal of practical experience with privatization in Great Britain, is more optimistic. He believes—strongly, in fact—that privatization will produce efficiencies even if a private monopoly takes control. Although he opposes monopolies of any kind, he thinks public monopolies tend to be worse than private ones.

To avoid possible problems associated with private monopolies—and even to avoid the burdens of continuing government surveillance—one should strive to create a competitive environment for newly privatized firms or services in which to operate. Consumers could then police quality and price, obviating the need for government bureaucratic surveillance.

This is a policy issue, as all discussion to this point has been limited to policy. If one wanted to try to institutionalize the benefits of these policies into a country's legal structure, then one would write *constitutional* rules requiring governments to do these things. For example, constitutions could be designed to simply outlaw the public provision of goods and services. At the same time, constitutional rules could be designed to allow the polity to express whether the private provision of goods and services should be financed solely through private means, or whether under certain conditions public finance or a mix of private-public finance could be used to finance the constitutionally mandated private provision of goods and services.

In the end, however, it may be that these economic issues have limited importance next to the much broader social and political implications of privatization. Manuel Tanoira, for example, underscores the need for dramatic reform of the attitudes that sustain mercantilism. In many parts of the world, especially in developing countries, governments must focus on development of stable, democratic political institutions. After all, without a stable political environment, no economic objectives for privatization or anything else mean very much. And here, for reasons given above, privatization may play an important role in helping developing countries build stable political and social institutions. It may do this by increased responsiveness to citizen desires—whether in the form of allowing people to own their own homes, or of expanding the range of citizen-consumer choices, or of general decentralized decision-making. These are the great contributions privatization may make to the search for progress in many parts of the world.

Further Reading

Recent popular articles about privatization in the Third World include:

James Brooke, "In Africa, a Rush to Privatize," *The New York Times,* July 30, 1987.

Donald H. May, "Third World Warms Up to the Private Sector," *The Washington Times*, February 28, 1986.

Peter Young and John C. Goodman, "U.S. Lags Behind in Going Private," *The Wall Street Journal*, February 20, 1986.

"Privatisation: Everybody's Doing It, Differently," *The Economist,* December 21, 1985.

"Privatization—A Route to Popular Capitalism?" *The Newsletter* from the International Center for Economic Growth, Fall 1987.

"The Catch in People's Capitalism," *The Economist*, October 3, 1987.

Recent publications on privatization in developing countries include:

Privatization: Policies, Methods and Procedures (Manilla: Asian Development Bank, 1985). Proceedings from a conference in Manilla January, 1985.

The High Road to Economic Justice: U.S. Encouragement of Employee Stock Ownership Plans in Central America and Caribbean, Report to the President and Congress, Presidential Task Force on Project Economic Justice (Washington, D.C., October, 1986).

Steve H. Hanke, ed., *Prospects for Privatization* (New York, Academy of Political Science, 1987).

Gabriel Roth, *The Private Provision of Public Services in Developing Countries* (New York: Oxford University Press, 1987).

Notes

6. Steve H. Hanke, "The Necessity of Property Rights

1. Adam Smith, *The Wealth of Nations* (Book V, Chapter ii, Part I).
2. Ibid. (Book V, Chapter ii, Part II, Article I).

7. Manuel Tanoira, "Privatization as Politics"

1. One of the most thorough and interesting accounts of this record is provided by Nathan Rosenberg and L. E. Birdzell, Jr. *How the West Grew Rich: The Economic Transformation of the Industrial World* (New York: Basic Books, 1986).
2. Quoted by Edward Shaw, in "The Search for Painless Privatization," *Buenos Aires Herald* (May 3, 1987).
3. An English-language edition of *El Otro Sendero* is scheduled for publication this year by ICS Press.
4. Jerry Jenkins, "Broadening Capital Ownership: An Initiative for Private Sector Production and Politics," prepared for an Agency for International Development conference on LDC Experience with Private Sector Development (McLean, Virginia: October, 1982), p. I-8.
5. P. T. Bauer, *Equality, The Third World, and Economic Delusion* (Cambridge, Massachusetts: Harvard University Press, 1981), pp. 103–4.

6. A useful discussion of this exception is provided in Gabriel Roth, *The Private Provision of Public Services in Developing Countries* (New York: Oxford University Press, 1987), pp. 195–229.

9. Steve H. Hanke, "Successful Privatization Strategies"

1. For a review of the theory of property rights and its implications for private versus public supply, see L. DeAlessi, "The Economics of Property Rights: A Review of the Evidence," *Research in Law and Economics*, vol. II, 1980.
2. U.S. General Accounting Office, *The Government Can Be More Productive in Collecting Debts by Following Commercial Practices* (FGMSC-78–59) (Washington, D.C.: Government Printing Office, February 23, 1979).
3. Joint Economic Committee, U.S. Congress, "Privatization of the Federal Government" (Washington, D.C.: Government Printing Office, 1984) p. 12.
4. W. Hsaio, "Public versus Private Administration of Health Insurance: A Study in Relative Economic Efficiency," *Inquiry*, December 1978.
5. D. G. Davies, "Property Rights and Economic Efficiency: The Australian Airlines Revisited," *Journal of Law and Economics*, April 1977.
6. D. G. Davies, "Property Rights and Economic Behavior in Private and Government Enterprises: The Case of Australia's Banking System," *Research in Law and Economics*, vol. III, 1981.
7. J. T. Bennett and T. J. DiLorenzo, "Public Employee Unions and the Privatization of 'Public' Services," *Journal of Labor Research*, Winter 1983.
8. E. S. Savas, *Privatizing the Public Sector: How to Shrink Government* (Chatham, N.J.: Chatham House Publishers, 1982).
9. C. B. Blankart, *Bureaucratic Problems in Public Choice: Why Do Public Goods Still Remain Public Choice*, ed. K. W. Roskampo (Paris: Cujas Publishers, 1979).
10. U.S. General Accounting Office, *Increased Productivity Can Lead to Lower Costs at Federal Hydroelectric Plants* (FGMSD-79–15) (Washington, D.C.: Government Printing Office, May 29, 1979).
11. R. S. Albrandt, Jr., "Efficiency in the Provision of Fire Service," *Public Choice*, Fall 1973.
12. B. Dowdle and S. H. Hanke, "Public Timber Policy and the Wood-Products Industry," in *Forestlands: Public and Private*, ed. R. T. Dea-

con and M. B. Johnson (Cambridge, Mass.: Ballinger Publishing, 1985).

13. Blankart, *Bureaucratic Problems in Public Choice*.
14. President's Private Sector Survey on Cost Control, *Report on Privatization* (Washington, D.C.: Government Printing Office, 1983).
15. President's Private Sector Survey.
16. President's Private Sector Survey.
17. Bennett and DiLorenzo, "Public Employee Unions."
18. J. R. Monsen and K. D. Walters, *Nationalized Companies: A Threat to American Business* (New York: McGraw-Hill, 1983).
19. Savas, *Privatizing the Public Sector*.
20. R. W. Poole, Jr., *Cutting Back City Hall*, Universe Books, 1980.
21. U.S. General Accounting Office, *Amtrak's Productivity on Track Rehabilitation Is Lower Than Other Railroads* (Washington, D.C.: Government Printing Office, 1981).
22. E. S. Savas, "Policy Analysis for Local Government: Public vs. Private Refuse Collection," *Policy Analysis*, Winter 1977.
23. H. M. Kitchen, "A Statistical Estimation of an Operating Cost Function for Municipal Refuse Collection," *Public Finance Quarterly*, January 1977; and W.W. Pommerehne and B. H. Frey, "Public versus Private Production Efficiency in Switzerland: A Theoretical and Empirical Comparison," in *Comparing Urban Delivery Systems: Structure and Performance*, ed. V. Ostrom and R. Bish (Beverly Hills, Calif.: Sage Publications, 1977).
24. U.S. General Accounting Office, *The Navy Overhaul Policy—A Costly Means of Insuring Readiness for Support Ships* (LCD-78–434) (Washington, D.C.: Government Printing Office, December 27, 1978).
25. C. Harrol, E. Henriod, and P. Graziano, "An Appraisal of Highway Maintenance by Contract in Developing Countries" (Washington, D.C.: The World Bank, March 3, 1982).
26. C. Feibel and A. A. Walters, "Ownership and Efficiency in Urban Buses," Staff Working Paper No. 371 (Washington, D.C.: The World Bank, February 1980).
27. Blankart, *Bureaucratic Problems in Public Choice*.
28. G. Roth, "Competitive Urban Transportation Services" (Washington, D.C.: The World Bank, April 16, 1984).
29. G. Roth, "Competitive Urban Transportation Services."
30. Feibel and Walters, "Ownership and Efficiency in Urban Buses."
31. Feibel and Walters, "Ownership and Efficiency."

32. M. W. Crain and A. Zardkoohi, "A Test of the Property Rights Theory of the Firm: Water Utilities in the United States," *Journal of Law and Economics*, October, 1978.
33. Bennett and DiLorenzo, "Public Employee Unions."
34. Everett G. Martin, "Successful Attack on Argentine Inflation Makes the New Economic Minister a Hero," *The Wall Street Journal*, October 9, 1985, p.34.
35. George Hatch, "Argentine President's Effort Fails to Streamline State-Run Firms," *The Wall Street Journal*, January 30, 1986, p.30.
36. S. H. Hanke, "Land Policy," in *A Mandate For Leadership Report: Agenda 83*, ed. Richard N. Holwill (Washington, D.C.: The Heritage Foundation, 1983).
37. S. H. Hanke, "Seizing Assets Slow and Subtle," *Reason*, November 1985.

14. Gabriel Roth, "Privatization of Public Service"

1. Gabriel Roth, *The Private Provision of Public Services in Developing Countries*, (New York: Oxford University Press, for the World Bank, March 1987). While recognizing the vital roles of the public sector in development, the Bank supports the vigorous encouragement of indigenous private sector enterprises in many countries because of their roles in mobilizing private savings, harnessing entrepreneurship, diffusing economic power, widening consumer choice, and stimulating competition. See A. W. Clausen, *Promoting the Private Sector in Developing Countries* (World Bank, 1985).
2. Robert J. Saunders, Jeremy J. Waterford, and Bjorn Wellenius, *Telecommunications and Economic Development* (Johns Hopkins University Press, for the World Bank, 1983).
3. *Journal of Commerce*, May 19, 1986.
4. "Public and Private Tubewell Performance: Emerging Issues and Options," Pakistan Subsection Report, South Asia Project Department, Irrigation I Division, (World Bank, 1983).
5. B. Kia, "Internal Financing of Water Supply and Sanitation in Developing Countries" (UNDP, Division of Information, 1981).
6. Clell Harral, Ernesto Henriod, and Peter Graziano, *An Appraisal of Highway Maintenance by Contract in Developing Countries*, 2d ed. (World Bank, 1985).
7. Gabriel Roth and George Wynne, "Free Enterprise Urban Transportation," (Washington, D.C.: Council for Internation Urban Liaison, Academy for State and Local Government, 1982).

16. Lawrence H. White, "Privatization of Financial Sectors"

Note: helpful comments have been received from Martin J. Anderson, Jerry Jenkins, Arthur Seldon, Robert Slighton, Michael Todaro, Bernard Wasow, and participants in the USAID International Conference on Privatization. Nonetheless they are all blameless for the views expressed here. A version of this essay appeared in *Economic Affairs* (August/September 1986).

1. The standard reference here is R. W. Goldsmith, *Financial Structure and Development* (New Haven: Yale University Press, 1969). See also P. J. Drake, *Money, Finance and Development* (New York: John Wiley & Sons, 1980), Chapter 3. A recent study is Woo S. Jung, "Financial Development and Economic Growth: International Evidence," *Economic Development and Cultural Change* 34 (January 1986), pp. 333–48.
2. See Ronald I. McKinnon, "Financial Policies," in *Policies for Industrial Progress in Developing Countries*, ed. John Cody et al. (London: Oxford University Press, 1980).
3. This point will be familiar to readers of Adam Smith, *An Inquiry into the Nature and Causes of the Wealth of Nations* (Indianapolis: Liberty Classics, 1981), p. 456.
4. This figure is for 1981–82. As of June 1982 only 6 percent of loans were being repaid on schedule. B. Wasow and B. Rahman, "Industrial Finance Policy," paper prepared for the Bangladesh Investment Incentives Study Unit (June 1985).
5. Cited by Chris Sherwell, "Indonesia's Successful Banking Reforms," *The Banker* (August 1985), p. 28.
6. Wasow and Rahman, "Industrial Finance Policy."
7. This has been stressed by Ronald I. McKinnon, *Money and Capital in Economic Development* (Washington: Brookings Institution, 1973).
8. Michael Blanden, "Bringing Greek Banking up to Date," *The Banker* (June 1985), pp. 33–34. Until recently the government dictated hundreds of different rates for different categories of loans.
9. See Drake, *Money, Finance and Development*, pp. 152, 221.
10. Drake, *Money, Finance and Development*, p. 181.

17. Steve H. Hanke, "The Anatomy of a Successful Debt Swap"

1. All indexes used in this paper are computed by converting values to U.S. dollars at the end of each year and then converting them to a base of 100 in December 1975.

2. Note that swaps can potentially inject money (cash) into the economy. This injection will occur if the original Chilean obligor is bankrupt or if the government is the obligor and the Banco Central provides the money. There is no injection if the peso proceeds come entirely from the original obligor. Also, redemptions in domestic debt are automatically "sterilized."

23. Steve H. Hanke, "Toward a People's Capitalism"

1. James Brooke, "In Africa, a Rush to Privatize," The New York Times, July 30, 1987.
2. Joseph A. Schumpeter, *Capitalism, Socialism, and Democracy*, 1942.

Contributors

ELLIOT BERG is president of Berg Associates, a consulting firm in Alexandria, Virginia specializing in international economic development. He was an assistant professor of economics at Harvard and professor of economics at the University of Michigan, where he directed the Center for Research on Economic Development. He has written extensively on labor economics, agricultural policy, and general development issues, and has served as an advisor to governments and consultant to international aid agencies including the World Bank and the International Monetary Fund. He was also a senior economics advisor to the Commission on Security and Economic Assistance (Carlucci Commission) in 1983.

MEHMET BILGIC is the director of privatization for the Turkish government's Public Participation Fund. Since July, 1985 he has been charged with carrying out privatization of state-sector entities. The Fund was created by Prime Minister Ozai to design and implement privatization of substantial portions of state-owned enterprises in Turkey. Prior to this, he served as a financial consultant to several food-processing companies and agribusiness projects in Turkey. From 1980–82, he served as financial manager for Turkish United Construction in Saudi Arabia. He also worked in the financial department of Profilo Holding, one of the largest manufacturers of durable consumer goods in Turkey.

ROSENDO J. CASTILLO is president of Forgues, Castillo Incorporated, a financial consulting and management firm. He has sixteen years of experience in international banking, working as an executive for the Bank of America in London, Canada, and Guatemala, and is presently a lecturer at Acusa Pacific University in Acusa, California, on issues surrounding the Latin American debt crisis. He is a member of the advisory board of the National Energy Extension Service.

L. GRAY COWAN is a consultant to U.S. government and private agencies on economic and political problems of developing countries. He is also the senior technical economic advisor to the Office of Policy Development and Program Review, Bureau for Program and Policy Coordination, USAID. He has served as a dean and professor of political science, Graduate School of Public Affairs at the State University of New York at Albany, and as professor of government and associate dean, School of International Affairs, Columbia University. He is the founder and director of the Institute of African Studies at Columbia University, and the author of numerous books and articles on Africa.

STEVE H. HANKE is a professor of applied economics at the Johns Hopkins University in Baltimore, Maryland, and chief economist at Friedberg Commodity Management Incorporated in Toronto, Canada. He is a member of the Presidential Task Force on Project Economic Justice, and a member of the Conseil Academique International of the Groupe de Recherche et d'Etudes sur la Privatisation in Paris, France. Professor Hanke served as a senior economist on the President's Council of Economic Advisors in 1981 and 1982, where he designed some of the Reagan Administration's initial privatization policies. Since then, he has worked as a privatization consultant to the U.S. Department of Housing and Urban Development, the U.S. Agency for International Development, the World Bank, and various private enterprises. In 1987 he edited a volume, *Prospects For Privatization*, published by the Academy of Political Science in New York.

PEDRO-PABLO KUCZYNSKI is the managing director of the First Boston Corporation and co-chairman of First Boston International. He was the Minister of Energy and Mines in Peru from 1980–82. Prior to that, he served as president and chief executive officer of Halco (Mining), Incorporated. He served in a number of capacities at the World Bank, including chief economist of the International Finance Corporation, chief of the policy planning division and chief economist for Mexico, Central America, and the Caribbean. He was also vice president and later partner, International Department of Kuhn, Loeb & Company International. He was a lecturer in economics at the Pontifical Catholic University of Peru. From 1967–69 he served as economic advisor to the president of Peru and as director of the Peruvian Steamship Company. He was also a senior economist, Western Hemisphere Department at the International Monetary Fund.

IAN MARCEAU is the senior economist and manager for Australian programs for Hassall and Associates, an international agricultural consulting company. Prior to moving to Australia in February, 1986, Mr. Marceau was a consultant on privatization to the Agency for International Development. He is the principal author of the 1984 report to AID on agricultural parastatals in sub-Saharan Africa. He also authored a 1985 report to AID on privatization of municipal service in sub-Saharan Africa. His present assignment includes advice to governments and the private sector in Australia and developing countries of Southeast Asia and Africa concerning privatization in agriculture and other economic sectors. He was formerly staff director of the Environment and Natural Resources Subcommittee of the U.S. House of Representatives and held policy positions in both the United States and Australia.

M. PETER MCPHERSON recently left his position as the Administrator of the United States Agency for International Development, and is currently the Deputy Secretary of the Treasury Department. He was also chairman of the board of the Overseas Private Investment Corporation. Prior to being appointed administrator of AID in 1981, Mr. McPherson served as Acting Counsel to President Reagan and General Counsel to the Reagan-Bush transition. He served on the board for International Food and Agricultural Development (BIFAD) from 1977 to 1980. He was also a member of the Joint Committee on Agriculture Development, a subdivision of BIFAD, and chairman of its Latin American Work Group. He was a partner and head of the Washington office of Vorys, Sater, Seymour and Pease, an Ohio law firm. As Special Assistant to President Ford, he assisted in the selection of presidential appointees, including ambassadors and judges. From 1969 to 1975, he was a tax law specialist with the Internal Revenue Service in the international corporate tax area. From 1964 to 1966, McPherson served as a Peace Corps Volunteer in Peru. There he coordinated the School Feeding Program and later worked in AID's Private Enterprise Office in Lima. He is a member of the bar association in Michigan and the District of Columbia.

LANCE MARSTON is the vice president and director of Government Consulting Services for the Hay Group, the world's largest consulting firm specializing in human resources. He has twenty-five years of government and business experience in strategic planning, cost/benefit analysis, manpower research, and procurement and contract administration involving alternative delivery systems for public services. For the past three years, he has directed several privatization projects, including a two-year assignment to establish a privatization program in American Samoa. He is now providing contract support for privatization initiatives being taken by other U.S. territorial governments in the Pacific. Mr. Marston has written a handbook describing the privatization process in American Samoa, and is currently preparing a guidebook on national and international developments in privatization.

TED M. OHASHI is a partner with Granville West Financial Services in British Columbia. As a chartered financial analyst with a major investment dealer headquartered in Vancouver through the 1970s, he was director of research and subsequently senior vice president. In these capacities he was a participant of the British Columbia Crown Resources Investment Corporation (BCRIC)—one of North America's largest privatization projects.

MADSEN PIRIE is president of the Adam Smith Institute, the London-based public policy institute. He and his institute have been at the forefront of the promotion of privatization in Britain. Privatization has become one of Prime Minister Thatcher's most successful economic policies. In the United States, Dr. Pirie has been on the staff of the House Republican Study Committee in Washington, D.C. and has been a professor of philosophy at Hillsdale College in Michigan. His books cover a wide range of subjects; they include *Trial and Error and the Idea of Progress*; *The Logic of Economics; Dismantling the State* and *The Book of the Fallacy.* He is also a former international general secretary of MENSA.

ROBERT W. POOLE, JR. is president of the Reason Foundation, a free market-oriented think tank based in Santa Monica. He serves as editor and publisher of its monthly magazine on current affairs, *Reason*, and is editor of three Foundation books: *Instead of Regulation* (1982), *Defending a Free Society* (1984), and *Unnatural Monopolies* (1985). In addition, Poole supervises the Foundation's Local Government Center, a research affiliate specializing in cost-cutting innovations in public service delivery. Poole has published extensively in periodicals on public policy, and is author of a handbook for the National Taxpayer's Union called *Cut Local Taxes—Without Reducing Essential Services* (1976), and a full-length book, *Cutting Back City Hall* (1980).

JOHN REDWOOD is a fellow at All Soul's College, Oxford, and a member of Parliament from Wokingham. He served as head of the Prime Minister's Policy Unit and was senior policy advisor on all social and economic policy. Presently he is the director of N.M. Rothschild and Sons and Norcross PLC, an industrial holding company. He is the author of several books on privatization, including: *Controlling Public Industries, Public Enterprise in Crisis,* and *Going for Broke.*

GABRIEL ROTH is a civil engineer and transport economist formerly with the World Bank. He is the author of *The Private Provision of Public Services in Developing Countries*, published recently by Oxford University Press. He has also worked for the Bank on matters related to transport pricing, planning, and deregulation. Prior to joining the World Bank in 1967, Roth worked in England as a consultant and as a research officer at the University of Cambridge. He was a Rees Jeffreys Fellow at the Road Research Laboratory. He is the author of *Paying for Parking, Paying for Roads, A Self-Financing Road System,* and (with George

Wynne) *Free-Enterprise Urban Transportation*. He is currently the president of The Services Group, a nonprofit organization that helps developing countries implement market-oriented policies.

DONALD SHAY is a vice president with the MAC Group, an international general management consulting firm that focuses on implementing strategic change in complex organizations. The MAC Group was formed in 1964 by Harvard Business School faculty and graduates and now comprises 150 full-time professional staff and 200 faculty from leading business schools in North America and Europe. Mr. Shay has fourteen years of consulting experience in business strategy, market planning, and most recently in privatization. He developed and helped to implement strategies for privatizing state enterprises in Jamaica and Grenada. His privatization work includes the evaluation of state enterprises, development of an overall strategic approach for managing the state enterprise portfolio, and the preparation of plans for marketing companies. Mr. Shay is a graduate of Lake Forest College, the Graduate School of Architecture at the University of Virginia, and Stanford Business School.

MANUEL TANOIRA is the former Secretary for Growth Promotion in Argentina, and now serves as Advisor to the President, with the rank of Secretary of State. Trained and experienced in industrial and systems engineering, Mr. Tanoira is president and director of several companies in Argentina. He owns a consulting and management firm in Buenos Aires that specializes in turning around ailing companies.

PETER A. THOMAS is currently a consultant with The Hay Group in Washington, D.C., where he specializes in international trade, public sector contracting, and privatization. During his career at Hay, Sears World Trade, and its management subsidiary, Harbridge House Incorporated, he has directed or been a key participant in many projects in which the focus of program operation and development has been the interaction of the public and private sectors. Mr. Thomas' recent projects have included assistance in privatizing a motorpool, a dairy, a marine railway, and an electric power system in American Somoa; the preparation of a "how-to" handbook for privatization; and the compilation of an eighty-page bibliography of worldwide privatization literature.

Lawrence H. White is an assistant professor of economics at New York University. He is the author of *Free Banking in Britain* (Cambridge University Press, 1984) and an authority on competitive monetary institutions. His articles on monetary liberalization and privatization have appeared in *American Economic Review* and other professional journals, as well as in numerous conference volumes. Dr. White has also acted as a consultant on monetary liberalization and on free banking zones.

Peter Young is currently executive director of the Adam Smith Institute's new U.S. branch in Washington, D.C. For the previous three years, he was head of research at the Adam Smith Institute in London, the public policy think-tank specializing in privatization policy. He directed the Institute's Omega Project, which produced fifteen separate reports containing privatization proposals for every area of government. Many of these proposals have since been adopted by the British government. He has written widely on privatization matters, and his work has been published by organizations such as the Heritage Foundation and the National Center for Policy Analysis as well as the *New York Times* and the *Wall Street Journal*.